THE FIVE-MINUTE CONVERSATION

Encouraging and empowering through brief encounters

ROY BELL

REGENT COLLEGE PUBLISHING
Vancouver, British Columbia

Published 2003 by Regent College Publishing
5800 University Boulevard, Vancouver, BC V6T 2E4 Canada
www.regentpublishing.com

National Library of Canada Cataloguing in Publication Data

Bell, Roy D.
  The five-minute conversation / Roy Bell.

Includes bibliographical references.
ISBN 1-57383-231-6

  1. Conversation—Religious aspects—Christianity. 2. Pastoral counseling. I. Title.
BV4319.B44 2003   253.5   C2003-910939-9

To Dr. Joyce Boillot,
family doctor, gerontologist
and a mentor in modeling
effective brief encounters.

ACKNOWLEDGMENTS

I am considerably indebted to Beverley Norgren, who deciphered my almost illegible handwriting. And to Elizabeth, my beloved wife and constructive critic, who carefully did considerable editorial work on the original manuscript as well as making valuable suggestions from her chaplaincy experience.

CONTENTS

INTRODUCTION

This book contends that the vast majority of
pastoral care in non-emergency situations takes
place in what appear to be brief, casual conversations.
These conversations frequently take place at the after-
service "coffee hour" common to many churches, but
certainly are not confined to that. They occur after all
kinds of meetings and seminars. They take advantage of
e-mail as well as the telephone. They include all styles of
casual encounters. This sort of pastoral care is not
limited to pastors, but occurs in chaplaincy work, parachurch work and lay ministry.

Such conversations frequently last five minutes or less.
Often the dynamics of the particular setting make them
even shorter, very rarely longer, though it must be
acknowledged, of course, that quite regularly the follow
-up will entail much longer interaction. Over any given
month a pastor will contact and hear a significant
number of people in brief encounters. The very nature of
life today, rightly or wrongly, creates a milieu in which
this is almost inevitable.

In spite of this there is little public acknowledgment of this as a reality. It is certainly not at first sight perceived as desirable and almost never thought of as something to be valued.

It is the most cost-effective way of being in contact with a congregation. Cost-effective can be understood as a purely secular attitude or a recognition of the importance of making every moment count in the service of the Lord.

If it is primarily thought to be a cheap and effective (in terms of time) way to do pastoral care, there will be few spiritual dividends. If it is valued as a way of ministering, then that can be different. The difference between these two attitudes will be a style of ministry that leads to cynicism and burnout, or a style of ministry that encourages and enlivens the body of believers and those in leadership.

There are skills to be learned and developed. There are spiritual gifts to be identified and enhanced. There are emotional as well as spiritual depths to be understood and sought.

Gerard Egan outlines at length the complexities of what is involved in becoming a "skilled helper." He points out that "priests and ministers are often the first to be sought out by people in trouble."[1] He lists what he describes as "the basic communication skills helpers need to interact effectively with clients at every stage and step of the helping process"—attending and listening, empathy and probing. He sees these as "essential human tools for developing relationships with clients and helping them move toward managing their problems in living."[2]

There is no doubt that acquiring and developing the skills Egan lists is a dire necessity for anyone involved in any kind of human interaction that goes beyond the superficial. Few people, if any, should be allowed into the pastoral ministry who have not learned to be the kind of skilled helper that Egan describes and develops.

It must be understood that the shorter the amount of time available for interaction, the more vital is the skill development required.. This book assumes and promotes the mastery of the skills that Egan advocates, along with their application to brief as well as longer interaction.

It also recognizes an important understanding of pastoral life. When someone in trouble first seeks out the pastor it is almost always in a casual setting. People need to check out the pastor to see if they receive an empathetic hearing. The brief contact is often a necessary prerequisite to a longer counselling encounter.

In addition, some people neither need nor want long-term counselling. They prefer the brief, apparently casual conversation. In these circumstances the pastor who has sought to acquire Egan's list of skills will be a powerful spiritual and emotional person.

More important than this, the pastor needs to be a person dependent on and conscious of the presence of the Spirit. The results will then be empowering and life enhancing.

All kinds of people will discover that a brief encounter can be a life saver.

The purpose of this book is not to abandon long-term counselling but to recognize brief encounters as valuable. This is seen in the practice of Jesus. It is valued in the context of a post-modern church. It has the potential to revolutionize pastoral care.

CHAPTER 1

CELEBRATING THE
FIVE-MINUTE CONVERSATION

How can any serious person believe that a brief conversation can be useful, let alone celebrated? What, of value, can be accomplished in such a short time?

It sounds like telling someone who needs brain surgery to take an aspirin.

Surely we have moved beyond the time when we assumed that a Bible verse and a short prayer would solve every person's problems, often without any attempt to clarify the problems.

When we promote the five-minute conversation as something that can empower and encourage, it would appear that we are trying to turn back the clock. If we seriously pursue this approach don't we risk reducing interaction to the very opposite of something that empowers or transforms?

There are numerous horror stories of troubled people going to a pastor or elder, burdened by a serious spiritual or emotional problem, and being dismissed in a few minutes without ever feeling heard.

The very idea of a useful five-minute session is, for many concerned professionals, anathema.

The purpose of this book is not to rehabilitate this rotten process. God forbid!

But perhaps in our anxiety to rightly reject "the Bible verse and short prayer" approach we have failed to understand the value of brief, apparently casual conversations. The effectiveness of a five-minute conversation depends not on the length but on what happens in that five minutes.

David Martyn Lloyd-Jones[3] was the premier preacher and pastor of the twentieth century in the English-speaking world, ministering before and immediately after the Second World War. Lloyd-Jones began his professional career in medicine and was at the top of the medical ladder when he believed God called him to pastor and preach. At Westminster Chapel in London he had huge demands on his time and skills. His biographer notes that on Friday nights and on Sundays he typically had a line up of at least ten people urgently wanting his attention.

He ran his "vestry meetings," as they were described, rather as a specialist would behave in his medical office. For the majority of visitors he would remain standing. His biographer claims that, unless it was a purely social visit, Lloyd-Jones would make an "instant decision as each person was shown into his room."[4] He is said to have asked himself these questions: "Was the person a Christian or a non-Christian? Was the problem spiritual or was there some indication that the individual had physical or mental problems requiring medical advice or treatment?"[5]

He would proceed to deal with the individual in the light of how he discerned the answers to his internal questions. Though he did give extended time to some people, the majority would receive five minutes or less, sometimes much less.

He was quite prepared to understand that, in some cases, the problem was psychological. In that event he would, if it was justified, conclude, "I doubt at this stage whether anything can be done about it."[6]

Surprisingly, in view of his alleged antipathy to psychology, he was bold enough to use its insight when necessary. A man, for example, who was severely troubled by blasphemous thoughts came to Lloyd-Jones with his problem. "He advised me (rather surprisingly) not only never to think about the problem again, but never to pray about it either. It was not really 'prayer' it was simply reminding myself of the problem."[7] Lloyd-Jones did see this person a second time but it would appear again to have been brief and effective.

Whether or not his questions were the correct ones, whether or not the time he gave was enough, whether or not his advice or counsel was accurate, few left his room without feeling heard. In addition to being heard they felt encouraged and empowered.

Was it the force of his personality? Was it the discernment that the Spirit gave him? Was it the very psychological insight that he would have often denied? Was it just because Lloyd-Jones was an exceptional, if not extraordinary person, gifted with unusual insight and spiritual authority?

In other words is it possible to generalize from Lloyd-Jones to the more ordinary pastor, parachurch worker, or elder?

One of C.S. Lewis's biographers, George Sayer, recalls an apparently casual conversation that provided major impetus to Lewis's search for God.[8]

Lewis and a fellow academic, T. O. (Harry) Weldon, were talking together. Weldon was, according to Sayer, "a cynic who scoffed at all creeds and almost all positive assertions."[9] In the course of the conversation Weldon made two very untypical comments. He said "there was good evidence supporting the historicity of the Gospels" and added, "Strange thing that stuff of Fraser's about the Dying God. It almost looks as if it really happened once."[10]

This so shocked Lewis that he re-examined the evidence in the Gospels and was forced to agree that "it was surprisingly good." The biographer goes on to add, "Jack re-read the Gospels and became more and more aware that they were not myths or made up stories at all, because the authors were simply too artless and unimaginative."[11]

Clearly nobody had a stop watch timing the conversation. But the significant part was brief. Weldon did not want to explore the issues he raised; indeed refused to do so.

Here we have a brief conversation that was dramatically significant for Lewis. It both empowered and transformed Lewis's life.

It is true therefore that, though brief conversations can have a highly negative connotation, the opposite is equally true.

Lloyd-Jones was certainly unusually gifted with insight far beyond the normal. There was also more involved in Lewis's conversion than the conversation with Weldon. What the two examples have in common is evidence that brief conversations can be crucial in God's plan and timing.

Why that should be any great revelation is itself surprising.

I have recently made a point of asking a large sample of people two questions. The first is to enquire whether they have ever had an extended conversation with someone, particularly with a spiritual leader, about serious personal issues. I was not concerned to know any details or with whom they had talked. Almost all had had at least one interaction of this sort but largely they would reveal that this was rare and exceptional.

The other question was whether they could recollect fairly brief conversations that were of critical importance. Invariably their eyes would light up, their responses would be immediate and affirmative. The majority, across gender and social position, could identify a specific conversation that had literally changed their lives. Some of these people had been believers for many years, others more recent. Across all age levels they reported conversations of five minutes or less that were a kind of epiphany.

Unmistakable, if anecdotal, evidence makes it clear that such occurrences as took place in Lloyd-Jones's vestry and in C.S. Lewis's college are part of human experience. They are universal. They are Christian in particular. They are not totally dependent on high or exceptional intelligence or remarkable insight.

There is, in fact, an enormous amount of human and spiritual conversation going on all the time in most people's lives. The variety in our day is immense. It can be by e-mail or fax, a telephone chat or a casual meeting in the mall or coffee shop. It can be after or during a church event.

While much of this interaction is, in some sense, superficial, it is often more than that. Rather than despising the so-called casual conversation, what we need to do is celebrate it. In addition we need to find ways of making it more effective and in the best sense more spiritual.

Hospital chaplains are trained to develop this particular skill, always avoiding the kind of professional gloss that frustrates rather than facilitates.

The pressures of the modern hospital are such that

time spent in the active treatment hospital is becoming brief indeed. One consequence of this is that the amount of time the patient can engage in longer conversation has almost disappeared. Chaplains must fit in a visit between all the other very legitimate activities. Five minutes or less is often the available time. It may never be enough, but it may be all they get. Good chaplains understand this and function in light of it. They seek to bring the caring and loving presence of Christ to the patient in the brief available time.

Though the time constraints are not exactly the same in pastoral ministry, there are similarities. In the social time that follows many church events it is rare to be able to give any individual person an unlimited amount of time. There may be exceptions, but normally two or three minutes is as long as a conversation is likely to last in that setting.

Can anything be accomplished in such a brief interchange? The answer may lie in the spiritual gifts and spiritual sensitivity of the pastor, and the capacity to listen, hear and focus. When there is a pastor so equipped effective ministry can and does happen.

Let me illustrate from my own experience.

It was Christmas. We had reserved a ship to tour Vancouver's waterfront and sing carols, a Vancouver tradition. Performing my pastoral duties, I was walking through the boat and came across a man in his late thirties, sitting by himself, looking exceedingly glum. I had seen him earlier with his wife, who had recently started attending church.

I introduced myself with a smile and said, "You look as if your wife dragged you here and you wonder why you allowed her to do so."

He immediately agreed and asserted quite vehemently that he had no time for Christians and Christianity. I responded that he was obviously a thoughtful and intelligent person who would not come to such conclusions without some attempt to examine the evidence.

He looked a bit sober. I pressed him further and asked what he had read recently. When it was clear that he had read virtually nothing, I suggested C.S. Lewis's *Mere Christianity*.

He grunted a kind of assent and I moved on.

Subsequently I noticed him attending church and was not surprised when he made a more formal appointment. His question was quite straightforward. "I've just become a Christian. What do I do next?"

That beginning contact took less than five minutes.

On another occasion I was walking from Carey Theological College to Regent College, which are affiliated. Catching up with a second-year student I noticed that he was not his usual cheerful self. I expressed concern.

The walk between the two institutions takes less than seven minutes. The amount of time left when I caught up with him was about half of that.

He was very open in telling me what was bothering him. It was clear that he had gone from an exciting first year to a miserable second year. We had a conversation about what was happening in his life that had produced this reaction. He shared freely some personal issues that had disturbed him. We talked them over and agreed to meet for a longer conversation.

The longer conversation and a time of prayer were important, but we would both agree that they would not have happened without the walk from Carey to Regent. That brief encounter proved to be a crucial intervention. Less than five minutes was enough time for us to clarify what was troubling him, for him to feel heard and to give him confidence that I cared enough to meet with him again.

Such brief conversations are clearly of considerable value. Almost every pastor or parachurch worker can recall productive conversations that lasted less than five minutes, as can the recipients of such conversations.

That is not to argue against long-term counselling but it is to underline that very brief, apparently casual conversations can be significantly helpful. Indeed they may lead to long-term counselling but that should not be the assumption.

Nor is it to argue that all casual conversations should lead to serious encounters. Exchanging informal social chatter is part of normal life. Discussions about work, family, sports, religion and current affairs are a natural part of human existence. Nobody would wish to turn every human interaction into serious discussion of life-changing matters.

At the same time, we seem in much greater danger of

ignoring the reality that people do have serious agendas. They are more likely to believe that nobody wants to hear them and resort to comparative trivialities because nobody cares, as they perceive it.

To go away from every occasion, whether it is church coffee hour or some similar encounter, without ever having a serious conversation is to reduce life to meaningless generalities and in many cases precipitates serious inner despair and acute loneliness with feelings of alienation.

When casual conversations touch significant spiritual, intellectual or emotional nerves, exciting things can happen.

One Sunday after morning worship I met up with an old friend I had not seen for some years. He gave every impression of being together spiritually and emotionally. The only apparent vulnerability was that he was facing serious surgery. When we touched on that his eyes filled with tears.

"That is not what troubles me," he blurted out. "You remember that accident," he recalled.

I had vague memories of what he was referring to.

"That has haunted me all my life since. I've never told anyone about this," he went on. For two or three minutes, while participants in coffee hour milled around, he poured out his soul. Then someone who did not know what was happening joined us, terminating the conversation.

My friend returned to ask that our conversation be confidential and moved back to his other contacts.

This brief, apparently casual encounter laid the groundwork for serious follow-up. It was something the man would not normally have welcomed but he was relieved to find a social setting where he could begin the process in an unthreatening atmosphere, where he could terminate the conversation any time he wished.

What was the value of such a brief conversation? It enabled him to test the reactions I would have to what concerned him. He had a sense of being heard and he did not even remotely feel judged. The contemplation of life-threatening surgery brought to the surface the long-ago accident for which he felt responsible and for which he had never been debriefed emotionally or spiritually.

Because my reactions demonstrated that I listened at real depth, it opened up for him the possibility of a more extended conversation where he could begin to expose how he really felt, admit his guilt and shame.

It provided some immediate emotional release. I could sense that happening even in such an almost-trivial amount of time. It was as if he had been consumed by the memories of the accident all these years and had felt obligated to conceal it. He could, at last, express the agony of the occasion and not feel compelled to deny it or minimize it. At least it opened the door to exploring the issues of guilt, shame and forgiveness.

Conversations such as this appear casual but are far from it. They often raise issues of immense importance to the individuals and their understanding of God and His ways.

Anyone listening carefully would find, on a regular basis, individuals only too willing to share the very deepest concerns of their lives. Such listening could signal the beginning of the end of those dark feelings of alienation that pervade our lives and leave us consumed by the conflicting feelings and beliefs that prevent us from living up to God's potential, let alone living lives useful to Him. No qualified person will contend that serious emotional and spiritual problems can all be resolved in five minutes or less. But five minutes can make a beginning. The aim is to find ways of making what appear to be casual encounters an appointment blessed by the Spirit.

The truth is that people in any leadership role in Christian work are under a great deal of pressure. This is true whether they have an official role or not. It may be true primarily of pastors and parachurch workers but it is also true of elders, deacons and many lay people who are perceived as wise and godly. Pastors, parachurch workers and lay leaders are unable to give long periods of time to enough particularly needy people.

What are they to do? Some argue that counselling is not an appropriate discipline for pastors and parachurch workers. The difficulty is that it is unavoidable. It is both natural and appropriate for people to turn for help to those they see as significant spiritual leaders.

There are at least two responsibilities that pastors,

elders and parachurch workers can assume. They can refer people to those with specialized competence to help. This, however, is rarely as easy as it sounds. To find local resource people who are psychologically competent and spiritually alive is a major frustration. Yet it needs to be attempted.

The other alternative is to find ways of providing short-term and exceedingly brief, insightful feedback to people—the five-minute conversation that encourages and empowers!

In my own ministry I have engaged in long-term counselling for which I am qualified. In addition I have developed a competent resource list of people to whom I have referred particular individuals.

It has only recently occurred to me that maybe the best contribution I have made has been the five-minute conversation. Often this would occur during coffee hour after the church service. Sometimes it would be in even more casual circumstances. On a street corner or between classes or on the telephone. Wherever it took place there were some common factors. It would last less than five minutes. Clarification would be vital. It would never be a monologue. There would be a high degree of empathy.

As I reread the Gospels I am amazed and reassured and refreshed to note that the brief conversation is a pattern sometimes followed by our Lord. With some rare and unusual exceptions, the dialogues recorded in the Gospels are quite brief. Granted, of course, Jesus possessed discernment that nobody else can match. Nevertheless, some measure of this has been given to his followers.

The belief that a great deal can be accomplished in very brief counselling is gaining some professional acceptance. Michele Weiner-Davis has popularized this viewpoint and has gained considerable recognition beyond the popular level. She argues against what she calls "antiquated, ineffectual ways of thinking about problems and how to solve them."[12]

She goes on, "I want you to know that there is a new way to find solutions—immediate solutions—to chronic problems that doesn't require you to analyse the problem to death."[13]

She boldly asserts, "I am in awe of how quickly people find solutions to complex problems or make momentous decisions that radically improve their lives."[14] She is an enthusiastic advocate of Solution Oriented Brief Therapy (SOBT).

I am not endorsing all that Weiner-Davis advocates. Nor do I wish to imply her support for what I advocate in this book. I simply assert is that faith in long-term counselling as compared with a much briefer variety is in serious debate among competent therapists and counsellors.

Weiner-Davis quotes Milton Erickson as an advocate of the belief "that change can occur quickly." He reasoned that since people can get sick suddenly, so too they can heal suddenly. He postulated that "lengthy treatment is less the result of intractable problems, and more the outcome of the therapist's self-imposed belief that rapid resolution of problems is impossible."[15]

For many people who do not have serious emotional problems, what appears to be casual conversation could at least open the door for solutions. Not everyone needs or desires long-term counselling, but everybody does need valid human encounters.

With the breakdown of family life a major support and resource is unavailable to many individuals. The virtual disappearance of the father in our society creates a huge need for legitimate and godly father figures. Whereas in the past a great many decisions and conversations would have been processed in the family circle, that happens less and less.

I find myself repeatedly coming back to the obvious question: Can we find a way to help pastors, elders and parachurch workers make use of the seemingly innocuous casual conversations to do more than discuss the weather?

The casual and brief conversations around coffee hour and its equivalents may be inadequate substitutes for the real support and accountability that the old arrangements provided, but they are considerably better than either nothing at all or a resort to the solutions that New Age advocates offer at a price too great to pay. New Age advocates are filling the huge need in our society for meaning and intimacy. Unfortunately they succeed in deepening the black hole instead of illuminating it.

Surely for Christian believers this need is a modern opportunity to fulfil Paul's injunction "Carry each other's burdens, and in this way you will fulfil the law of Christ" (Gal. 6:2). To be an empathetic listener whose heart and mind is open to people, to give someone your full attention, even for a very few minutes, is a gift of surpassing value.

Without this, Christian fellowship is a mockery. It simply promises what it does not deliver. A consequence of this is to increase alienation and cynicism. Its active pursuit is to open the door to intimacy and Christian love.

CHAPTER 2

WHAT CAN HAPPEN IN FIVE MINUTES OR LESS?

The curse of modern church life is that what passes for personal contact is too often banal and empty. Instead of decreasing personal feelings of alienation, it often increases them. When the conversation focuses on almost everything else in the universe except that which is closest to the heart of the particular person, the result is largely negative.

There is so much of this in ordinary secular life that church involvement should not imitate it. If, in fact, that is what happens, church then becomes a breeding ground for cynicism and despair. Anecdotal evidence on this is clear.

The cynic concludes that church experience and church people are no different from anyone else. Worse than that, they profess to be different and fail to deliver.

Worse still, such banality inadvertently reinforces the fear that God Himself is like that. If those who profess to know Him and represent Him are fundamentally indifferent, how can anyone believe that He cares?

Despair is very close to the surface in the lives of many people who come to church. It may be argued that the local church is not the cause of that despair. Even if that is true the pastor, in the preaching, too often raises the expectation that the gospel significantly deals with despair.

When the conversation, by its superficiality, in effect reinforces the despair, the wound to the soul is serious indeed. Raising expectations only to deny them is unproductive and destructive.

It does not have to be so.

What can we realistically expect to happen out of these brief conversations?

It is important to acknowledge that five minutes is woefully inadequate if someone is facing a major personal catastrophe. However, leaving aside the more serious traumatic experiences, and allowing for good referral skills when that is clearly necessary, there is substantial anecdotal evidence that five minutes or less can be enough time for something significant to happen.

This can take place on at least two levels.

In the first level helpful information can be exchanged.

Contact: My sister, who lives in another city, is getting married. She has been through a divorce. Do you know any evangelical pastor in that area who would marry them?

Pastor: It happens that the Baptist minister in that city is quite generous on that kind of issue. If she contacts him, he will give her a hearing. It sounds as if your sister retains her evangelical faith. Do you know whether she has talked to anyone about what went wrong with her marriage? The issue of remarriage is more complicated than simply finding a sympathetic pastor. I am sure you know that.

Contact: I know that and so does she. Would your friend counsel her, if she asked?

Pastor: He might. He would also know someone to whom she could be referred, if they both thought that was appropriate.

Contact: That would be excellent. Thank you.

In a healthy church or parachurch organization, the pastor, or the equivalent, will be a vital resource like this. Good networking is one feature of a good church.

In addition to the exchange of information, the manner and content of the exchange makes or breaks the pastoral relationship. This, of course, carries implications of long-term damage or long-term growth in Christ.

It needs to be understood both spiritually and psychologically that any time a person feels heard and cared for significant things happen in that person's life. To be blunt, they feel better about themselves and they can feel touched by the love of Jesus.

That may seem extreme but all the anecdotal evidence confirms it.

It is clear that when a healthy, even if brief, exchange takes place good things happen. The pastor, elder or parachurch worker at least gets to understand something of what is going on in the person's life beyond the superficial. The person perceives that.

In those brief moments when pastoral worker and a contact start a conversation two people connect. In those few minutes enough can take place to either assure the parties that a relationship can profitably be established, or, in fact, confirm the opposite.

If the encounter takes place following the pastor's sermon and pastoral prayer it may build on that. The contact's comment may be very tentative, but by what is said or unsaid significant information will be exchanged.

Contact: I was intrigued by what you said this morning about anger.

Pastor: You found that part of the sermon interesting.

Contact: Yes, interesting is not a strong enough word. I'm not sure what word I feel is appropriate.

Pastor: (with a smile) You find the topic of anger important and interesting but you are not quite ready to describe exactly in what way?

Contact: That's true, but I confess that anger is an issue for me. I feel guilty when I am angry yet I don't often get angry, and only when it is justified.

Pastor: It sounds as if this is a concern for you. Would it be helpful to talk more about this sometime?

Contact: I would need to think about that, but thank you for the offer.

Up to this point the pastor knew very little about the contact—largely size, shape, gender, age, occupation. This conversation, however, begins a process of understanding and relating that moves the relationship forward and deeper. They can begin to develop a bond of shared intimacy that may lead to the individual beginning to trust the pastor with what is really going on in her life.

The contact is obviously taking a fairly big risk in acknowledging that anger is a personal issue for her. That implies considerable trust as well as risk.

The pastor may be pushing her faster than is probably wise, but at least he is not ignoring her or diverting her from the point she wants to make. He has not insulted or patronized her. He has opened the door without forcing her to follow up until she is ready.

If, instead of asking for more time, she had responded in greater depth, the pastor might have discerned that her situation required that she be referred to someone with specialized training. However, if the pastor rushes to refer her without sufficient time for her to be heard, she may see it as rejection.

This might be an alternative scenario.

Contact: Yes I would like to talk with you. I come from an abusive background. But nobody in or out of the church wants to hear my pain and anger. It just never goes away. It seems to get worse instead of better.

Pastor: It is painful in the extreme to come from an abusive background. When you feel rejected by God's family it must make it much worse.

Contact: Yes, you've sure got that right.

Pastor: I would like to hear about what has happened to you. I don't know if I can help you, but I would like to make an appointment with you. When we've done that maybe we can agree about follow-up

Contact: I would really like that. How do I make an appointment?

A consequence of this interchange is clear. Her feelings of alienation will begin to melt and real dialogue commence.

"Feelings of alienation will *begin* to melt." The emphasis has to be on the word begin. For someone with her history it will likely be a prolonged process. But even to reverse her feelings that nobody wants to hear her pain and anger is a solid start. If she and the pastor have some time together when she really believes she has been heard, that will be a step forward. If they agree on the appropriate skilled helper and if the pastor continues to follow up with her to discover what progress she is making, real dialogue has begun.

It is difficult to exaggerate how important such an apparently brief conversation can be to someone like this woman. She likely appears to be someone who has her life together. There may be nothing in the way she presents herself that would suggest a complicated background. A consequence of this could be a pastor's too-easy assumption that all is well.

The skills exhibited by this pastor are immense. He shows discernment; he is a spiritually sensitive person. He has a feeling that there is more involved than appears at first sight. Such feelings are not be universal. They are a gift of the Spirit. They must not be ignored.

There is more here. The pastor is attending carefully to her. He is not restless, he is not wanting to close off the conversation and move on to someone else. He does not appear distracted or attempt to distract her.

He is quite up front with her. His response is, "It is painful in the extreme to come from an abusive background. When you feel rejected by God's family it must make it much worse." The genuine empathy this displays is quite exceptional and heart warming. There is much more communicated here than a few pious words.

Another obvious gain will be that the individual will feel that the quality of time given is genuine. She begins to feel cared for and esteemed. This should result in some increased sense of self worth.

She has acknowledged an abusive background. Obviously this needs to be explored. The pastor restrains his curiosity. The abuse can be catastrophic or relatively minor. It is certainly real to her and a more confidential appointment has to be arranged.

What has happened in those few minutes is that someone, at last, is willing to hear "her pain and anger." That will not, by itself, heal the effects of the abuse. It will, however, give her a glimmer of hope and restore a sense that the pastor sees her as someone worth his time.

The real test of the value of the brief conversation between this person and her pastor is her perception that the pastor is someone who genuinely cares for her. That he sees her as someone worth spending time with and conveys this by words and attitudes. People pick this up very quickly. They may sometimes be wrong, but mostly they know intuitively and spiritually whether or not the pastor cares for them.

But without doubt it will take place only if she perceives the pastor as someone who gladly gives time to her. That time must make up in quality what it may lack at that moment in quantity.

If she were to respond to her pastor's enquiry about her readiness differently, the process would be different.

> **Contact:** I do find the topic of anger interesting and intriguing. It is not really a big issue for me. I do feel badly, however, for people whose anger seems to me to be fully justified. Could you do a follow-up on that someday? What outlet do they have that does not produce feelings of guilt?

> **Pastor:** That seems worthwhile to me. Maybe you could think about that and let me have more of the kind of questions you think should be addressed. One way or another I will work on it. You could fax me or e-mail if that would work for you.

> **Contact:** That would be great. I will do that.

Mother Theresa would argue that something much more elevated is also going on here. In some sense Christ will minister and be ministered to as in Matthew 25:40: "And the king will answer them, Truly I tell you, just as you did it to one of the least of these who are members of my family, you did it to me."

In many ways there is a bigger question that must always be at the heart of pastoral care. It goes beyond the matter of motivation—Why am I doing this? It transcends the question, Am I being helpful? or Do I care? It is always a theological question, Where is God in all this?

It is not only asking myself the question, What would Jesus do? And Mother Theresa is right when she argues that it is not just something I do *for* Jesus. It is ministering *to* Christ as well as ministering on behalf of Christ.

The pastor or elder who takes Matthew 25 seriously is functioning in a very different world from that of clergy self-help advice and general good will.

The enemies of quality pastoral care are many. But high on the list are trivialization, secularism and a lack of biblical and theological content and motivation. It may seem unfair, even unreal, to put the burden for reversing these on the quality of the conversation in casual encounters. But where else can such a change be made?

The effectiveness of the preaching will largely be measured by the way in which the love and caring it advocates is implemented. To a large extent this will be assessed by the behaviour in church encounters. Where else? If all that goes on there is conversation that majors only on trivia, what other conclusion can be drawn other than that this is the style and content of pastoral care in this church?

Another danger is when only secular responses are proposed. All kinds of trauma begin to come out in focused casual conversation. In this person's case it is an abusive background. What does she mean by abusive background? Does the pastor have awareness of what is helpful in handling abuse? Does the pastor have anything to offer in addition to or as an alternative to secular methodology?

It is impossible not to have a theological rationale for pastoral care. It will either be a biblical model or end up with trivialization or secularism. When pastors, elders or parachurch workers, through having little or no biblical or theological basis for how they function, default to a secular model they are depriving themselves as well as the people like this person of where Jesus is in all of this.

A Matthew 25 model would at least be a place to begin. Because the pastor's heart's desire is for Matthew 25 to take place the whole mind set changes as will the effect of the dialogue and the sense of job satisfaction.

What we need in general pastoral care is a paradigm change. Social events are not just a time "to work the room." The point is not to just make casual contact and thus assume knowledge of the problems and cares of the congregation. That is not to assert that none of that is of any value. But if that is all that is in the pastor's mind and heart, it will in the end be self defeating to all concerned.

The congregation will eventually come to the conclusion that the pastor is not really a spiritual person. They may not want a pastor who is overly pious and legalistic, but they do need one who is spiritual. To be dismissed as lacking the very quality that defines the office is tragic for everyone.

In addition, the pastor's sense of job satisfaction will diminish and be replaced by cynicism and unhappiness. When you add to that some of the other negatives there may be in church life, it will be difficult to avoid serious burnout along with emotional and spiritual withdrawal.

The reality is that the number of people that a pastor with the best of intentions can see on a more formal counselling basis is less than five per week. Even if the pastor is willing and capable of doing formal counselling, it will soon be recognized that the time that can be allotted is very limited.

The pastor can very quickly discover that it is very easy to spend ninety percent of the time allotted for counselling on five percent of the church population. The result is that many people who could benefit from counselling simply get little or nothing.

This is further complicated by the fact that the five percent who consume all the time are often exceedingly needy people who do not always make the kind of progress that the time investment should justify.

The pastor must decide on a way to relate to the congregation as a whole in ways that are productive. In the modern church this is done through the regular preaching and teaching; it is fulfilled by seminars and workshops on issues as varied as spirituality, anger management, depression, Alpha, marriage and family opportunities. Indeed Michael J. McManus in *Marriage Savers* has supplied material and a critique of wonderful alternatives to the sad stories of marriage and family breakdown in its modern expression.[16]

But nothing replaces personal pastoral contact. In the midst of these workshops and seminars all kinds of personal interaction take place. In the course of a Saturday workshop the pastor will have a number of very brief conversations. These will interact with what the church member perceives are the personal implications. Issues will be raised that are of life-changing significance. The pastor with good listening skills and genuine empathy will have very special encounters.

Pastoral ministry is not about being nice. It is not about patronizing the inadequate. It is not even about ingratiating oneself with the more prominent church members. It is about serving Christ. It is about ministering for Christ and in some sense to Him.

If, in all good conscience, five minutes or less is all we have, it is a more than legitimate prayer that some of that ministry will happen. Instead of dismissing brief encounters as superficial and irrelevant, we need to see them as part of the very bone marrow of pastoral relations.

They either set positive things in motion or stymie them. They are not a substitute for longer time spent but they are a kind of parallel operation. If we enter into them prayerfully and with an ear open to the Spirit, they become moments when the sweet presence of the Spirit can begin His transforming work. Being open to this can be the new beginning to a transforming ministry and profound understanding of effectiveness in ministry.

A very great deal can happen in five minutes or less. It was life changing for Matthew and Nathaniel among others. It has been radically significant for many people over two thousand years, including Augustine. To give up on this is a denial of the work of the Spirit. To affirm it is to praise God for being at work in our day and every day.

CHAPTER 3

ADDRESSING SOME
UNDERLYING ISSUES

W hy is it that occasions of genuine connection with needy people, instances of people feeling understood and beginning on the path of healing, do not happen more often? A simple, direct answer is that it is because of a failure of expectations.

It is a sad and tragic reality that in too many churches people do not expect anything supernatural to take place. We have all the vocabulary of faith but little of the experience. When we anticipate little or nothing, little or nothing is the consequence.

The account of the seven churches in the Book of Revelation makes this melancholy point. This culminates in the miserable diagnosis of the church at Laodicea. "You are neither hot nor cold." When the local church, for whatever reason is indifferent, it is an organism that reproduces the same.

In such an atmosphere, spiritual and emotional, the

Spirit is essentially forbidden to do His work. How different it is in a worship service that is spiritually alive and vibrant. Even in a church like that of Corinth it should be possible to discern that "God is really among you" because "the secrets of his heart will be laid bare" (1 Cor. 14:25).

In such an atmosphere people will be sharing at a level that goes far beyond the sterile and the secular. When the famine of expectations ends, the hunger for God surfaces.

A second set of reasons why such ministry does not happen more often is that the pastor lacks spiritual insight, has little, if any, capacity to focus or attend to particular individuals, is fearful of being discovered to have no answers, or simply does not understand human dynamics.

Some of this is a failure of the way in which pastors are educated and some is a lack of the fundamental spiritual gifts that enable spiritual ministry to take place. The education of the pastor rightly focuses on developing cognitive understanding of the faith. Too often, however, it simply enlarges the Christian vocabulary without deepening the experience of God in Christ.

It begins at theological college regardless of the particular theological bias. In one of his Alpha courses Nicky Gumbel recounts how the influence of the theological college made him reluctant to be specific about the claims of Christ. It was undoubtedly not the intention of that particular institution.

There is an urgent need for both pastor and church to pray Paul's awesome prayer for the church in Ephesians 4:14-21. The prayer includes such fundamental promises as "power through his Spirit in your inner being," "rooted and established in love," "to grasp how wide and long and high and deep is the love of Christ" and "able to do immeasurably more than all we ask or imagine."

When pastor, chaplain, lay leader or parachurch worker is praying this prayer wholeheartedly it is hard to imagine that conversations will be other than alive and vital. The contacts, as a result, will have less difficulty in being heard when they open up with a significant problem. The leaders' fears of being found inadequate will begin to fade because they are no longer solely dependent on their own insight and resources. Listening, anyhow, is more important than solving. Acceptance of this will reassure and revolutionize pastoral care.

It would, however, be unfair to the pastor and church to maintain that all the negative causes lie at their door. Some responsibility is that of the person in need. For a whole complicated and complex set of reasons many people find it very difficult to open up to anyone. Though they must accept some responsibility for this, the church must do all in its power to create an atmosphere where the person who is insecure and afraid is made to feel loved and cared for. This is almost always mediated by the extent to which real listening is perceived.

It needs to be emphasized again that listening is vital to helping people make any progress in resolving issues. Indeed, often the very fact of being heard may be as valuable to the person as the attempt to resolve the problem itself.

It is no accident that James expects us to be "quick to listen, slow to speak, slow to become angry" (James 1:19).

This is in stark contrast to the seminary professor who is reported to have continued typing his latest book while a student attempted to pour out his heart! There appears to be more here than the professor's anxiety to meet his publishing schedule. The capacity or lack of capacity to listen is a spiritual matter. It communicates an indifference to the student's needs and indeed to the professor's sense of call.

Pastors may not act as obviously as that professor did; but when they signal indifference, by whatever way they choose, they are in defiance of the clear word of Scripture.

The capacity to listen also raises the whole question of the pastor or parachurch worker's own spiritual life. Tragically it may be more absent than present. Why is it that pastors and church workers find it so difficult to cultivate a personal spiritual life? Recognizing its importance while failing to follow through on it is more the norm than the exception. Though my evidence for this is anecdotal I believe it to be accurate.

It is not a case of simple indifference. By and large, it is an interest in and a concern for the Christian life that leads people into ministry. This makes it a bigger puzzle.

It would be understandable, but too simple and superficial, to blame the people they serve. From the Corinthian church to the present day, churches have put severe emotional pressure on those they appoint—and just as quickly challenge—as leaders. That has not changed over the centuries.

Ministry is clearly one of those "total institutions" that too easily devour their leaders. There has never been a week in all my years in ministry when I could believe I had fulfilled all the tasks that others expected or that I demanded of myself. A "total institution" is one that takes over the whole life of its participants. This, for the pastor, includes emotional and spiritual factors. Donald Capps quotes the typical pastor's lament: "I have no life outside the parish."[17]

Though this is true, the problem does not lie so much with what the institution does to its workers, as with how the worker reacts to what the institution is perceived as doing.

We need a radical rethinking of why most of us react to our circumstances as we do. Ask any pastor who is or has been in trouble and you will get an explanation of what is perceived to be the cause. It is almost invariably something the church or some powerful individual or clique has done. "Everything I do that is wrong is someone else's fault" is a not unfamiliar refrain. That it is sometimes justified can lead us to believe that it is always justified.

Not so!

Albert Ellis is closer to the truth when he argues that people mainly feel the way they think. In other words the problem lies not so much in the circumstances but in how I react and, especially, how I think about those circumstances.

That is consistent with Jesus' statement, "Out of the heart come evil thoughts" (Matt. 15:19). The direct application of this passage may be to "evil thoughts, murder, adultery, theft, false testimony, slander," but the implication is surely that the source of evil thoughts is not so much in external factors, but in the human imagination and will.

The cognitive behavioural therapist is in support of this when contending that it is not so much the *activating event* that causes the emotional turmoil but the person's *belief system*. The argument is basically straightforward. My reactions to any crisis are a function of my belief system, not simply the nature of the crisis. If my belief system is healthy, that will go a long way toward modifying the way I react. It will also keep me from spending countless hours and days unearthing who and what is to blame.

In other words, it is my belief system that dictates my emotional and behavioural reaction and influences my spiritual life.

This has enormous consequences. At first sight, people in pastoral ministry would appear to have a healthy belief system. After all, they are well informed biblically and theologically. But the reality is they have considerable difficulty in internalizing that set of beliefs.

Their theological beliefs are too often overwhelmed by their emotional makeup.

Shad Helmstetter sums it up in his provocative book *What to Say When You Talk to Yourself.*[18] He argues that the biblical passage "As a man thinketh so he is" often reflects a negative reality because, if what we think about ourselves and our world is essentially negative, we end up in emotional difficulty.[19]

As he puts it, "We've got a bad program! We have been trying to achieve our goals with our own on-board computer pre-programmed to hold us back." He lists an intriguing set of examples of "frequently used negative self talks." "It's going to be another one of those days." "Nothing ever goes right for me." "I can never afford the things I want."

Gerald Corey takes it to another level when he quotes Albert Ellis: "People condition themselves to feel disturbed, rather than being conditioned by external sources." Ellis goes on to argue that "humans are self talking, self evaluating and self sustaining. They develop emotional and behavioral difficulties when they take simple preferences (desires for love, approval, success) and make the mistake of thinking of them as dire needs."[20]

What is being argued here is of considerable importance in asking why effective one-to-one ministry does not happen more often. It is not only because of spiritual inadequacies, it is also because of the way both the pastor and the contact process what is happening.

The cognitive behavioural therapist would say that a defective belief system distorts what is going on and results in emotional disturbance.

> **Contact:** You know my mother. I got a phone call from her last Wednesday. She is sure she has breast cancer. It is an awful shock to us all. Just when things were getting easier this happens.

> **Pastor:** I don't blame you both for being so upset. The very thought of cancer scares me. Why don't we pray about it?

Aside from the almost improbable ineptness of this exchange, it is clear that all three—pastor, the contact and his mother—have a belief system about self diagnosis as well as a near phobia about cancer. Because their belief system is so strong, they have the poor woman scheduled for death and disaster when an accurate diagnosis has not even been made!

The pastor is a co-conspirator with the beliefs of the contact and the mother. Until they change that belief system, little else will change.

> **Pastor:** Your mother is afraid she may have cancer. Could you encourage her to have it checked out? It's difficult not to react to the very word cancer, but until she gets a diagnosis we can't be sure about it. Can you get her to do that? Could I be of any help to her and to you?

The pastor here is gently challenging the belief system of both the contact and the mother.

Another way of understanding this is to accept that an understanding of human dynamics can be helpful in pastoral ministry as long as it does not replace the spiritual element.

Pastors need to discover the healthy theology that is found in Scripture and use it when appropriate to correct negative self talk. The process of doing that will influence how a person feels about the stresses of life and will help the person take responsibility for emotional and spiritual well being.

It would be idle to pretend that this is easily accomplished. Indeed, it may require some professional help. A negative belief system seems to come with mother's milk and is hugely difficult to shift, but that shift needs to happen.

One way of correcting negative self talk is to begin by writing down what the person says to himself or herself when anything negative happens. Unfortunately, that is rarely something of a positive theological nature. Usually it is a self-destructive revelation. Ellis argues that emotional disturbance is fostered when "it is fed by the illogical sentences that the person continually repeats to himself or herself, such as 'I am a miserable failure, and everything I did was wrong. I am a worthless person.'" Ellis repeatedly makes the point that "you mainly feel the way you think." Disturbed emotional reactions such as depression and anxiety are initiated and perpetuated by the self-defeating thinking.[21]

Identifying the negative thinking is only the beginning. Correction requires that the person make an attempt to think through alternatives that are biblically healthy, accurate and relevant, as well as life affirming. That will be a challenge. Examples of these for the pastor would be: "I make mistakes like all human beings but by God's grace I have helped some people make significant progress in their lives," or "Nobody is a worthless person in God's eyes; everyone is precious to Him as am I." When the pastor has a healthy belief system it will be contagious.

Reinforcing the alternatives will be a vital step in beginning to discover a different view of God, of life and of oneself—surely one element in the beginning of real spirituality.

But it is equally clear that it is only a beginning.

We must make all kinds of efforts to recover and develop a deep biblical spirituality. Any particular choice will doubtless depend on one's personality and ecclesiology. But the process must begin and be extended.

Maybe some simple, straightforward questions would be a starting point.

1. How aware are you of the diversity of Christian resources to help you develop your spiritual resources for today's world?

52

2. Who serves as your resource person or spiritual guide and mentor?

3. Does that person hold you accountable as well as give you support?

4.Is he or she capable of doing both?

5. Do you have people in your church who pray specifically for you and your so-called casual conversations?

6. What attempts are you making on a regular and systematic basis to deepen your love for and attachment to Jesus?

7. Is the issue of spiritual warfare a reality for you?

8.How are you coping with that?

Healthy ways of responding to these questions will help the ministry worker enhance self understanding and deepen relationship to Christ. It will also enable the worker to begin to hear other people and respond more profoundly.

What we want to identify and change is the negative, destructive belief system out of which too many people, including pastors, function. In so many cases that is where the beginning of change must start.

The contact was an attractive young woman, intelligent and professionally successful. She had a strong cognitive faith. In spite of all of this she was troubled. She responded quite bluntly to a her pastor's general enquiry about how she was.

Contact: I am frustrated because no man I like is attracted to me. What's wrong with me?

Pastor: You feel that the reason you do not have a male relationship is because there is something wrong with you?

Contact: Well yes, I suppose so. Other women who are no more attractive than I am have no difficulty. There's something wrong with me.

Pastor: Let me get this clear. You think that the reason men do not react to you is because there is something wrong with you?

Contact: Absolutely, I think they see me as an overeducated, stuck-up woman with a chip on her shoulder about men.

Pastor: You sound as if you believe it is possible that how you think about yourself and your thoughts about yourself frustrate you in forming a healthy male relationship. Is that a possibility?

Contact: You're putting it back on me. Are you saying that the problem lies in how I view myself? How can that help me?

Pastor: That is something worth exploring if you would want to do that.

Contact: I'm ready to explore anything that would help. What do you suggest?

This is a pretty pushy conversation that seems justified only where there is already a good relationship. It is also a conversation with someone who can handle the ideas that are under discussion.

The contact will even enjoy discussing the part that her belief system plays in her male interactions. She may even respond to Albert Ellis. Her life may change!

This brief conversation at least opens up a whole new set of questions she needs to explore.

It raises, and to some extent answers, the questions we are continually asking.

It is not just important to understand the value of such brief encounters. It is vital to perceive that the spiritual and emotional life of the pastor or elder and the church itself is of fundamental importance.

CHAPTER 4

A CHECKUP ON YOUR FIVE-MINUTE CONVERSATION SKILLS

If you are going to take seriously this concept of conversations lasting five minutes or less, it would be important to get a handle on some beginning skills. These are in addition to, but not a substitute for, personal spiritual depth.

The checkup offered here is a way to begin that process. The ten questions are designed to raise the profile of common do's and don'ts.

As you work through it you should become more self aware and more open to the Spirit. The objective is to discover your own strengths and weaknesses. It will be better to work on the questions in the order they are presented. You might find it helpful to do some role playing with someone who is concerned about quality care.

Breaking old habits and forming new ones is a challenge. The payoff will not only be the way the Spirit uses you in other peoples lives, but it will also be in the sense of satisfaction this brings you. In addition, your capacity to give and receive intimacy will grow. That is a considerable reward. These questions, it should be clear, are only a beginning.

1. When you have a casual conversation do you make sure it remains casual and does not get serious?

Yes_____ No_____

2. If someone gets serious do you match his or her story with your stories?

Yes_____ No_____

3. When you become involved in a casual conversation with someone you consider boring do you keep surveying the group for someone more interesting?

Yes_____ No_____

4. Are you in such a hurry that you habitually finish the other person's sentences?

Yes_____ No_____

5. Do you find yourself asking questions designed primarily to satisfy your own curiosity?

Yes_____ No_____

6. Are you satisfied with listening primarily to the words being spoken rather than the underlying feelings?

Yes_____ No_____

7. Are you quick to offer solutions to the problems you perceive being expressed?

Yes_____ No_____

8. In casual church settings do you look around for people who seem anxious for personal contact and avoid them?

Yes_____ No_____

9. Do you assume that if a person appears emotionally and spiritually "together" he or she really is together?

Yes_____ No_____

10. If and when you feel prompted by the Spirit to talk to somebody, do you dismiss the idea as unlikely and much too dangerous?

Yes_____ No_____

Anyone who answers No to all ten questions is much too good for this cruel world. Alternatively they might ask someone who really knows them for confirmation or amendment!

Anyone who answers Yes to all ten questions needs to re-examine priorities in life and review relationships. That person almost certainly should not be in pastoral ministry.

I do not know what would represent a "normal" score, but any Yes answers should be an incentive to work for change. It would certainly mean that this book is for you!

The more Yes answers you turn into No answers, the greater your usefulness and your sense of satisfaction in the relationships God gives you.

THE IMPLICATIONS OF THIS CHECKUP

1. When you have a casual conversation do you make sure it remains casual and does not get serious?

I'm convinced that pastors and other Christians involved with people need to build on the so-called casual conversation that they engage in every day. The ten-question checkup is designed to highlight ineffective and unproductive ways of doing this. The opposite is equally true. Every time you do the opposite of what a particular question suggests (i.e. answer No), good things can happen.

I'm not suggesting that every casual conversation should be manipulated or upgraded to a life-or-death concern. Yet in a perfectly natural fashion this will often happen if it is allowed to.

Pastor: It is great to see you back in church after your vacation. I hope it went well.

Contact: Thank you for your concern and welcome back. The vacation did not go as well as we had hoped.

Here is a very natural conversation that has the potential to become serious. The pastor could cut it off, as too many pastors do:

Pastor: Too bad the vacation was not so great. But it is good to see you back in church today. I hope next time it goes better!

Or the pastor could encourage the conversation to go deeper:

Pastor: You sound as if the vacation was a bit of a disappointment.

Contact: Yeah! That is an understatement. We went to see my wife's parents. That was a huge mistake.

With the first response the pastor robbed the contact of the opportunity to unload some serious frustrations. The second response opened the door. There is an obvious problem with his in-laws; there is a possible problem with his marriage. If these concerns are not surfaced and to some extent clarified, serious pastoral problems loom large.

2. If someone gets serious do you match his or her story with your stories?

The second question illustrates the tendency of pastors to allow themselves to lapse into anecdotage.

Pastor: I'm sorry to hear of your grandfather's death. Were you close to him?

Contact: Yes, I loved him very much and I'm having difficulty dealing with my anger over his sudden death. I really need him.

Pastor: I remember when my grandfather died. I felt exactly like you do. But with time I recovered and I'm sure so will you.

The pastor is guilty of gross insensitivity. Among other things is the assumption that the pastor's experience of the death of a grandfather is identical to that of the other person. It never is. May God deliver pastors from premature "anecdotage."

The pastor could have responded in a way that would have given the person the chance to open up if she wanted to.

Pastor: You loved your grandfather a great deal and your loss of him is so troubling that it makes you feel angry. You sound like someone who is going through understandable grief and also is bothered about feelings of anger.

Contact: Yes, that's about it. I do feel angry. Sometimes I feel guilty about that. Is it wrong to be angry?

Pastor: The Bible actually says, "Be angry," though it adds, "and sin not." That's a hard combination. I would give yourself permission to be angry. If it persists, I'd be glad to talk with you about it. Would that be okay?

Contact: That would certainly help.

3. *When you get involved in a casual conversation with a boring person do you keep surveying the group for someone more interesting?*

It is not unusual to find yourself committed to a conversation with someone you perceive as dull and uninteresting. However, such a categorizing of any person is absolutely contrary to how Jesus perceived people. It ought to be rejected, and indeed, genuine repentance is appropriate. Such categorization is also very superficial. There is nobody more important at that moment than the individual to whom you are responding.

4. *Are you in such a hurry that you habitually finish the other person's sentences?*

The answer to this question reveals more of the pastor than the pastor may desire.

The habit of finishing other people's sentences is, at the very least, a sign of gross disrespect and impatience. It probably is also a measure of hidden anger. It will likely provoke resentment. A wife whose husband habitually finished her sentences responded to him, "I don't like you finishing my sentences for me. Ninety percent of the time you are accurate, but even then I prefer to finish my own sentences—thank you all the same."

5. Do you find yourself asking questions designed primarily to satisfy your own curiosity?

Asking questions that reflect curiosity about someone else's private life is highly inappropriate. The other person will be rightly offended and will begin to withdraw. It is therefore both wrong and contra effective. If you find yourself doing this, it would be desirable to examine your motivation.

6. Are you satisfied with listening primarily to the words being spoken, rather than the underlying feelings?

This is the acid test of whether the conversation, whether short or long, has the potential to be effective. There is much here to be concerned about. Egan, in *The Skilled Helper*, writes at length about attending and listening. Picking up the non-verbal cues is a skill that requires experience and sensitivity. The capacity to see beyond words must be seen as an essential human survival process. There are those who can, those who find it difficult and those who are willing to learn.

Egan points out the vital importance of this. "We know from experience that even when people are together in silence, the atmosphere can be filled with messages."[22]

It is clear that to be able to read the other person in any social situation is important. It is absolutely vital when there are severe limitations imposed by lack of time. In such circumstances it is obviously important to find a way to encourage that person to confirm, deny or amplify.

> **Pastor:** You seem to me as if you've had a difficult week.

> **Contact:** A difficult week would be a very inadequate way to describe it. How did you know?

> **Pastor:** You just don't seem to be your usual self. Also, I could not help overhearing your conversation with Jack and it sounded as though you were not hearing each other very well.

> **Contact:** Jack is very kind, but he doesn't always pick up what I am trying to tell him. I find that frustrating sometimes.

The pastor is certainly very direct. That right may have been earned and in this case the contact does not resent it. In the conversation between Jack and the contact it is very different. "He does not always pick up what I am trying to tell him"!

It would be beyond reality to expect Jack ever to pick up on silence. The pastor, however, should be able to read the individual with whom contact is being made.

Egan goes on to say, "Sometimes the facial expressions, bodily motions, voice quality, and autonomic physiological responses of a client communicate more than words."[23]

To tune in to all of that is a very tall order. It is not a beginning skill. Egan carefully points out, "There is no simple program available for learning how to read and interpret non-verbal behavior."[24]

However, the very awareness of its value and importance will be a good start. Egan is clearly nervous of drawing attention to the value of reading non-verbal cues. He emphasizes nevertheless that "a failure to keep non-verbal behavior in context, distorts their reading of the client and the client's problem situation."

It is vital here that the pastor not be content to accept only the words being spoken, especially if they appear to contradict what is clearly visible.

Pastor: You seem as if you have had a difficult week.

Contact: No, my week has been just fine.

Pastor: You wouldn't lie to me, would you? (With a warm and caring expression.)

Contact: (Eyes filling with tears) I've had a horrible week.

For the pastor to be as aggressive as this is to take considerable risks. It could be justified only in a long-term trusting relationship. It is obviously dependent on an accurate reading of all the non-verbal cues. Even at that, only a pastor who has had good training and can communicate non-verbally all the empathy needed should attempt such a response.

However the pastor handles the situations that arise in casual conversation, a capacity to be dissatisfied with only the words being spoken is a *sine qua non* (without which nothing).

Question six should also raise matters of gender. The sex of the pastor or parachurch worker will affect the relationship. By and large men and women listen and react differently. An awareness of this is clearly important. So serious is this that it challenges the long-held assumption that male pastors are the appropriate people to counsel the opposite sex.

This is not the primary concern of this book but it does need to be raised and seriously pondered. Is the baggage of the counsellor so overwhelmed by gender that it makes the relationship too complicated? When long-term counselling is necessary, gender must be seen as a significant factor.

Counsellors, sacred or secular, who are uneasy with their own sexuality or who are uncomfortable with that of their clients should not be involved in counselling. At a very minimum they should interact in a serious way only with those who do not stimulate them sexually.

7. Are you quick to offer solutions to the problems you perceive being expressed?

This question is directed toward the person who always knows how to solve other people's problems right away. Hearing may be dull, listening skills may be absent, the problem may not even be identified, but that person knows the answer. What a pain!

> **Contact:** We're having a difficult time with our teenage daughter. She is quite rude and defiant. It has thrown the family into chaos and has put stress on us as a couple.

> **Pastor:** It is quite normal to have trouble with teenage children. She will grow out of it. I wouldn't worry. Just commit it to the Lord.

The pastor does not yet know what constitutes being "rude and defiant." It could be relatively minor or close to catastrophic. The church member has not described what "chaos" means. Is the stress in the marriage minor or major?

All these need to be clarified. That will not happen in these circumstances. There are alternative responses.

Pastor: You sound as if you are all having a difficult time and you seem to identify your teenage daughter as the cause.

Contact: Yes, it does feel like that, though I suppose there is more to it. Her defiance is not really all that out of line. Maybe we are overreacting.

At least the possibility of some real dialogue is emerging. It may be possible to have some sense of the extent of the problems and go from there.

8. In casual church settings do you look around for people who seem anxious for personal contact and avoid them?

There are few working pastors who are not aware of people in church who are chronically anxious and want some time with the pastor at every available opportunity. It is a fine art to give such a person some time without being monopolized and being unable to speak to others. That it is difficult to deal with is unquestionably true. Ignoring it will simply increase the problem. One way of responding to the chronically anxious is to reply warmly.

Pastor: I know you are going through a difficult time. Would it be okay if I give you a phone call early in the week?

Contact: I would really appreciate that. You will be sure to do it, won't you?

Pastor: Yes, I will.

The pastor will need to follow up on the promise.

On the other hand, the person who is not normally demanding but is clearly anxious needs to be contacted right away and some attempt must be made to discover the cause or causes.

Pastor: I get the impression you are feeling a bit troubled this morning.

Contact: Yes, I suppose so; but that's life for lots of people isn't it.

Pastor: Yes, I think that's true. Can I ask you if there are particular reasons for you to feel troubled this morning?

Contact: I do have some things on my mind, but they are pretty trivial.

Pastor: They may seem trivial, but if you're feeling upset it might be important enough for you to talk about it.

Contact: Well, you know all the talk about downsizing in the company I work for? Well, on Friday I got downsized.

Pastor: That does not sound trivial to me. Can you tell me more?

Contact: Yes, I'd like to, but it is kind of personal. Could you find some time this week to have a coffee or lunch? There are too many people around here.

Pastor: Yes, I sure can. Let's check that out now.

The truth is that the pastor has spent enough time in these circumstances to identify a substantial reason for that individual's anxiety. If the pastor had not done that, the person would have gone home even more distressed than in the beginning.

9. Do you assume that if a person appears emotionally and spiritually "together" he or she really is together?
This question is a two-edged sword. Nobody appreciates a pastor who is always playing the amateur psychologist. To have someone in a spiritual vocation who is constantly probing is not welcome.

However, the pastor who continually takes appearance for reality is not an improvement. There are lots of Christian people who work hard to appear "together" when inwardly they are falling apart.

Pastor: You're looking great today!

Contact: Are you suggesting that I don't look so great some days?

Pastor: No! Not really, but I expect you have days when you are up and days when you are down. I certainly do.

Contact: You do! Well, to be honest, so do I. But nobody likes someone who is always down in the mouth.

Pastor: Maybe not, but I think we need to give ourselves permission to have a bad day and not force ourselves to be hearty and cheerful.

Contact: You're right. I need to think about that. You're saying that nobody should force themselves to act and look cheerful all the time. But is not that how a Christian should look— always on top of things?

Pastor: It does not quite fit the description of either our Lord or Paul.

Contact: That's interesting. Let me chew on that and take it up with you again some day soon.

Not a particularly earth-shattering conversation but at least the beginning of a more authentic relationship.

*10.If and when you feel prompted by the Spirit to talk to
somebody, do you dismiss the idea as unlikely and much too
dangerous?*

In some ways this question is the most important. It
basically draws a line in the sand. It distinguishes the
pastor who is little more than a good secular counsellor
from the pastor who is in touch with the Spirit.

Undoubtedly there is a need to differentiate between
impulsive reactions and listening to the Spirit. There is a
world of difference between the pastor who, however
cautious and tentative, seeks to hear the Spirit's voice
and the pastor who sees that as irrelevant.

James S. Stewart, the famous Scottish preacher and
teacher of the mid 20th century, would pray through a
page of his church directory every day. My own
experience of doing this is that a name or names would
be drawn to my attention as I prayed. I would follow up
with a phone call that would simply be a friendly call.
Invariably out of that call would come a serious issue.

Pastor: I was going through the church directory
and just felt like giving you a call to see how you
are doing.

Contact: I appreciate your concern. This is, to
tell the truth, not one of my better days.

Pastor: By the sound of your voice you are
having a tough day.

Contact: Well, you know we lost a baby a number of years ago.

Pastor: I did know about that. It is not something that a parent would ever forget.

Contact: Thank you for understanding that. People don't know how to react to us. By and large they expect us to have gotten over it.

Pastor: Getting over it is not very easy.

Contact: The particular issue is that today would have been her birthday. You could not have called at a better time.

This conversation is going to exceed five minutes and will involve a time of prayer. It does, however, illustrate the importance of listening to the Spirit and being available to Him.

These ten questions certainly do not exhaust the issues raised by casual conversations. They do, however, highlight major concerns. The big concern is how to change one's mindset and practise going from Yes to No.

It would be idle to assume that this happens easily or quickly. It involves considerable self awareness. A simple exercise would be to sit down after some social occasion and review in your mind the conversations in which you participated.

Hopefully there would be some that were social and light hearted. Even with those it would be vital to ponder whether you might have missed something. It would be interesting, even salutary, to use the questions as a check list. For example, if there were no serious conversations, that would tell you something. If nobody raised any "big ticket" items, it is likely they did not feel they were given permission to do that. What does that say about that church or organization?

Casual conversations can become spiritual realities if the pastor has committed himself to the Spirit for Him to guide and direct during social occasions. It would be valuable to ask spiritually minded people to seek the Spirit's direction not only for the pastor but for themselves.

The greatest challenge in pastoral care today is to keep spiritually fresh and alive. Rather, it is to allow the Spirit to keep me fresh and alive. The insight of the secular psychologist is invaluable, as are some of the techniques and procedures. Paul was bold enough in conversation with the Stoics and Epicureans at Athens to quote their poets (Acts 17:28). It surely legitimizes reference to Carl Rogers or Michelle Weiner-Davis.

Nevertheless, the insistence of the New Testament is always on being "spiritually minded" (Rom. 8:5-8). Almost any pastor will be aware of the mine field this represents. Well-meaning people claim to be in touch with the Spirit and uncritically offer advice that becomes catastrophic.

The pastor and lay people whose gifts are endorsed by responsible believers should not be in that category. Whatever risks may be involved, the risk of ignoring the Spirit should be impossible to contemplate.

CHAPTER 5

DEVELOPING YOUR FIVE-MINUTE CONVERSATION SKILLS

The history of pastoral ministry is littered with the casualties of highly intelligent pastors who were unable to relate to or understand ordinary people. One of the great puzzles in pastoral ministry is the lack of correlation between intelligence and the capacity to pastor. The tragedy is that some full-time Christian workers lack insight.

The new emphasis on emotional intelligence may be of considerable help in enabling us to understand why this is so. Daniel Coleman has written extensively on this.[25]

He defines what he means by emotional intelligence and helps us understand that intellectual and emotional intelligence are different not just conceptually but "express the activity of different parts of the brain. The intellect is based solely on the workings of the neocortex, the most recently evolved layers at the top of the brain. The emotional centers are lower in the brain, in the more ancient subcortex; emotional intelligence involves these emotional centers at work, in concert with the intellectual centers."[26]

If Coleman is correct, we are dealing with two very different kinds of intelligence, coming from and utilizing different parts of the brain. On the basis of this model we can understand the previous puzzle—why otherwise bright people are sometimes inadequate in human relationships.

There are also obvious implications for the selection and training of Christian leaders.

Coleman criticizes the failure of business to recognize this. He states categorically, "Our research reveals deplorable weaknesses in how businesses train people in skills; from listening and leadership, to team building and handling change."[27]

If this is true for business it is even more true for people in Christian leadership.

Coleman defines emotional intelligence as "the capacity for recognizing our own feelings and those of others, for motivating ourselves, and for managing emotions well in ourselves and in our relationships."[28] Assuming Christian convictions and beliefs along with Christian character, there could hardly be a better description of the essential skills needed for any kind of people ministry.

Understanding and working through the issues presented by Coleman would be of great value to anyone involved in pastoral ministry. He lists what he calls the "five emotional and social competencies."[29]

These competencies are basic for anyone working with people. They are particularly vital for those involved in very short-term conversations. Because there is less time available, the skill level of the counsellor needs to be higher.

Coleman draws attention to self awareness, self regulation, motivation, empathy and social skills.

It is encouraging and hopeful that he believes emotional intelligence can be developed. "Unlike IQ, which changes little after our teen years, emotional intelligence seems to be largely learned, and it can continue to develop as we go through life and learn from our experiences."[30]

An awareness of the need to grow in this one area of life would be a beginning step. Making use of the resources Coleman sets out in *Working with Emotional Intelligence* would get a person going in the right direction. Openness to a good spouse would also be a place to begin. It might both indicate the extent of the problems, if any, and, hopefully, provide encouragement and support.

In assessing and developing one's five-minute conversation skills, a first necessary insight is a suspicion of one's own ability to form a speedy diagnosis. In other words, the individual who is seen as the care giver must never be quick to make definitive judgements. It is virtually impossible to be able, in five minutes or less, to make even a semi-educated guess at what the other person is really concerned about. To keep an open mind, however, is not the same as being uninformed or unaware.

In one of the first counselling courses I attended, the professor, whom I knew to be an incredibly perceptive person, informed the class that he spent as much time resisting his diagnosis as he did believing it.

My immature reaction was one of total disbelief. I felt even that he was not being as straightforward as he should be. How could he, with his skills, believe that? I felt little inhibition, at that time in my life, in drawing immediate conclusions when I counselled someone.

If my teacher was right about drawing premature conclusions when doing longer-term counselling, how much more important it must be when having very brief interactions.

The reality is that it is for the client to inform the counsellor, not the other way around. A consequence of this is that the most vital human skill is the capacity to listen.

James is very concerned that those to whom he is writing obtain what he calls wisdom. "If any of you is lacking in wisdom, ask God, who gives to all generously and ungrudgingly, and it will be given you" (James 1:5).

He emphasizes one of the marks of this wisdom: "You must understand this, my beloved: let everyone be quick to listen, slow to speak, slow to anger" (James 1:19).

Pastors and parachurch workers are not famous for being "slow to speak," or known for being "quick to listen." Admittedly, it is difficult with all that education not to give the benefit of it to anyone within reach! However, if the information that is so generously made available is almost entirely irrelevant or premature, it will not be received in the spirit in which it is offered.

Genuine listening skills are difficult to acquire. Peter Davids comments on James 1:19, "The content of the proverb is simply that one ought to listen carefully and neither speak rashly nor get angry, advice as wise now as then."[31]

Alas, theological training gives little attention to listening skills, and models them even less. Whole courses are devoted to preaching and communication, but little is taught or demonstrated on the value and skill of listening.

The importance of listening is not a modern discovery. I was fascinated to find out how central listening is in the Benedictine approach. "Listen" is the first word of St. Benedict's rule for monasteries. Kathleen Norris speaks about "listening for the irruptions of grace into one's life—often from unlikely sources."[32] While listening here is primarily listening to God, it must surely equally be applied to human-to-human relationships.

Could it be that we can and should expect that not only will listening be a gift to the person to whom you are relating, but a very real gift to you as well? Would this save pastors from endless anecdotes and illustrations that likely have little or nothing to do with the life situation of the person in front of them?

I am listening not simply as a favour to that person, but by listening I may discover an "irruption of grace." My own experience would confirm this, but it also rebukes me for those many times when the quality of my listening was inadequate and therefore unproductive. The consequences of this were not only a failure to minister in any appropriate way, but considerably less gain or growth in myself. Do I hear Mother Theresa again making an even more awesome reminder that I failed to minister for Christ and to Christ?

Anecdotes are rarely, if ever, a source of ministry. When an individual is severely burdened and needs to be heard, anecdotes can be considerably destructive. Individuals who are trying to find a way to unburden serious concerns are distracted by a story that likely has no relevance to the situation. It is not their story anyway. They become frustrated by the lack of perception, they close up shop, lock the door and pull down the shutters.

In the meanwhile the pastor moves to the next victim, unaware of the fallout. She or he may go blundering on to inflict the same deaf ear on someone else. The one opportunity the needy person was hoping for that morning is lost. The person leaves feeling more deeply the alienation that has come to govern life in that situation. It is clear then that biblical teaching, monastic practice, professional training, along with personal experience, all confirm the importance, the value, indeed the absolute necessity, of learning how to listen.

This, of course, is also the reiterated theme of the

counselling movement. From Carl Rogers et al, the heart of any attempt to counsel is almost invariably rooted in the capacity to listen. It is an expression of "unconditional positive regard." To put it more negatively, a failure to listen is an assertion that one's own agenda is more important than the other person's.

The most effective way to communicate that you care for someone is to listen at depth. It involves a number of quite specific skills. It requires, for example, a willingness and an ability to set aside one's own agenda and ego needs and to focus on the other person.

This is challenging at the best of times, but is particularly difficult following a public occasion when the pastor has been speaking. The rush of adrenaline is so great that the pastor, often concerned to get positive feedback, will find a way to move on quickly to someone who will satisfy the almost overwhelming need for affection, attention and approval.

The question that needs to be addressed is quite straightforward: Do I have the capacity and desire to focus on the needs and agenda of another person for whom I have spiritual responsibility? The whole heart of ministry is to care deeply for those whom the Lord has entrusted to our care. It is both a biblical and emotional expectation.

Gerard Egan has written helpfully on these concerns from a largely secular viewpoint.[33] He quotes Rogers on empathetic listening. "It means entering the private perceptual world of the other and becoming thoroughly at home in it. It involves being sensitive, moment by moment, to the changing felt meanings which flow in this other person, to the fear or rage or tenderness or whatever he or she is experiencing."[34]

That is quite a tall order. It is easy to dismiss it as too ideal or to regard it as impossible in the context in which short-term encounters take place.

Maybe it is legitimate to argue that it is close to ridiculous to apply such a standard to an interaction of five minutes or less.

Maybe, but it does focus on the heart of any productive human interaction. Can I give other people the kind of empathetic listening that will enable them to believe that, for whatever length of time we have, they have my full attention in the most profound way?

Other people manage to do this. The busy family doctor does it. However full the waiting room may be, you expect, and hopefully get, the doctor's full attention once you are face to face. The paramedic does it. The trauma doctor does it. The good sales person does it.

For centuries a vital element in Catholic pastoral care has been the rite of confession. Though the use of confession has seriously declined, it still exists. When it was a normal part of church life it was, at most times, quite brief. It was intended to be anonymous. In the confessional the individual seeking pardon and forgiveness was physically separated from the priest; there was only voice contact.

My concern is neither with the content of the exchange nor with the theology behind it. It is to point out that for those who came, truly penitent, it was often both a spiritual and an emotional release. In addition it was a brief encounter. Often the exchange would last less than five minutes.

It can, in all fairness, be argued that many who came to confession could have benefitted from a much longer process. Whether or not that is accurate, it is clear that for many centuries this brief process was a central and effective element—and indeed a means of grace—in that church. This is not to argue that it was appropriate to allow pastoral care to be almost monopolized by confession. But it is simply to recognize that spiritual and emotional benefit has been mediated in comparatively brief periods of time in many contexts.

Whatever the motivation, there are people in addition to the priest at confession who come close to Roger's ideal. Is the pastor going to be the exception?

It is impossible in the scope of this book to look at these important issues in detail. Fortunately, Egan does this for us, complete with a workbook. He includes some fascinating questions. For example, he asks, "How intently do I listen to what the client is saying verbally, noticing the mix of experiences, behaviors and feelings?"[35] It is difficult to check this out. An effective—but maybe risky—way of finding out is to check with your spouse. Another way would be, after some social interaction, to reflect on how often you moved the conversation from the other person's agenda to your own.

Which leads us to another question Egan asks. "What

distracts me from listening more carefully? What can I do to manage these distractions."[36]

In rereading the Gospels I am staggered by Jesus' capacity to focus. He could do this regardless of the pressures that were closing in on Him. For example, Luke 22 records an enormous number of relationships and events leading up to His arrest and trial.

It includes Judas arranging for the betrayal of Jesus, the physical arrangements for the Passover, the debate over who should be considered the greatest, Peter's bombast, the inability of the disciples to stay awake and pray, and the battle with the Prince of Darkness.

It is astonishing that He could focus on Judas when it was appropriate and on Peter with his personal ego. In the middle of the horrendous events in His own life, he refused to be distracted from the situation facing His disciples.

In contrast, how easily and quickly we pastors, elders and parachurch workers become distracted. Often it is by our own emotional needs. Sometimes it is the desire or perceived need to touch base with as many people as possible. Occasionally it is anxiety that the person we are talking to will dump anger and frustration on us. It can also be that we see the person as unimportant to our view of life and the world and the local church.

Whatever the reason, and there are many more, distraction is the name of the game.

This is not to ignore the reality that there will be lots of occasions when it is appropriate to say, "I think I hear your concerns but I don't think we can deal with them right now. When would be a good time for us to talk? How can we do that? It is important to me for that to happen."

It is equally acceptable to respond by saying, "I think what you are concerned about needs someone with more skills than mine. Can I get back to you with some suggestions? Would you be comfortable with that?"

What is not acceptable is to brush off a needy person because the person does not seem significant to you.

Jesus' longest reported conversation is in John 4 when He spent time with the Samaritan woman. He evidently valued her enough, in spite of her public reputation and lack of social position, to do that. He did not brush her off, even though she was a social and ethnic reject.

The New Testament makes no bones about its objection to those who rely wholly on human wisdom as the substitute for spiritual insight. Paul bluntly insists that "God chose the foolish things of the world to shame the wise" (1 Cor. 1:27). He goes on to add, "My message and my preaching were not with wise and persuasive words, but with a demonstration of the Spirit's power, so that your faith might not rest on men's wisdom, but on God's power" (1 Cor. 2:4).

Instead of what he describes as "human wisdom," Paul advocates reliance on the Spirit. In particular he insists that believers must be "taught by the Spirit," otherwise they "cannot understand." They must be possessed by spiritual discernment.

Discernment—that is, the gift of the Spirit—must be seen as crucial.

Whether Paul is dismissing all human insight or setting out priorities can be debated endlessly. What is beyond debate, however, is his assertion that to function without the Spirit is a denial of the very heart of the gospel.

There can be few pastoral issues where the need for spiritual discernment is more urgent or more vital than in short-term conversations. Reliance on spiritual discernment surely does not give licence for ignorance of human dynamics. Nor does it give permission for superficial reactions that hide behind spiritual arrogance. It seeks to go beyond these.

Leon Morris argues, "Paul is insisting that the person whose equipment is only of this world, the one who has not received the Holy Spirit of God, has not the ability to make an estimate of things spiritual."[37]

He is not commenting on the man or woman who rushes to give advice arising out of personal belief in the possession of the gift of discernment. The least one would expect is that before any spiritual gift is claimed or exercised, it would have the confirmation and endorsement of significant Christian believers.

Gordon Fee says that "discern," in this passage, has to do with making "appropriate judgements about what God is doing in the world."

Clearly the priority of the gift of discernment is crucial for anyone who is sought out for advice and counsel. To rely only or mainly on counselling techniques and human wisdom would be to shortchange the seeker, to deny the person the very spiritual insight and resources that are so clearly needed.

This does not imply that the huge resources and insights that are available today should be dismissed or trashed. But it surely means that to go about one's business as a pastor, elder or spiritual director without reliance on the Spirit's gift of discernment is unacceptable.

It is clearly no simple issue. There are some well-meaning believers who consider themselves to have immediate insight from the Spirit that enables them to move from diagnosis to prescription to cure at the speed of light.

One such person will blithely say, "I have a word from the Lord." Some of those who profess to be able to know what the problems are in five minutes or less may have an exceptional gift. Even if they do, some caution would be highly desirable. Such an exceptional gift would require clear and unequivocal confirmation and endorsement from mature believers. Without such backup no credence would be given and indeed people should be warned against such practitioners. This needs to be emphasized again and again.

Dr. Martyn Lloyd-Jones was a highly qualified medical doctor and he did not despise his training and the expertise it gave him. Nevertheless, he possessed and sought spiritual insight that transcended those gifts. He was gifted by the Spirit with the capacity to grasp a person's concerns and make relevant and godly observations.

To quote Gordon Fee, he could "make appropriate judgements about what God is doing in the world."[38] Those judgements were both personal as well as cosmic.

Few are equipped like Lloyd-Jones, but there are people in the Christian community who are gifted by the Spirit with the insight and analytical skill that blesses those they counsel.

Truly godly discerners are those who listen with a "third ear." They take in all the other evidence: body language, emotional expression, verbal statements and more. But they also listen to what the Spirit has to say. They are not quick to make judgements. They are reflective more than prescriptive. They have learned to be both suspicious of what they think they hear and open to it.

Ironically, they are often people who are willing to learn from so-called secular sources. They will not give such sources the dignity of Holy Scripture, but they will not dismiss them cavalierly.

The kind of things that need to be absorbed in developing your five-minute conversation skills are as follows. In the first place, develop a willingness to listen to all that is being shared. This requires both a capacity to be aware of one's own emotional and intellectual reactions and the ability not to be governed by them. An awareness of the temptation to make quick judgements is vital. More than anything else, listening to what the Spirit is saying in the situation must always be the priority.

It may very well be that what the person with discernment believes the Spirit is saying is not compatible with all the other insights. In that case short-term counselling should be set aside. If the concerns raised by the client and by the Spirit are of serious consequences the person will obviously require unthreatened time. In that case, addressing the issues cannot be done in five minutes or less and should not be attempted.

What must happen is that the person doing the sharing will feel that he or she has been heard. It is this capacity to listen that should be prized by both parties. It is therefore legitimate, and indeed highly desirable, for the pastor to restate to the person what she believes she heard in order for clarification to happen. Gaining confirmation or correction is clearly vital.

To be heard and to be able to confirm, amend or deny what the counsellor heard is satisfying and surprisingly affirming. It creates a climate of trust and intimacy. All of these are essential elements in any relationship of value.

The one skill the pastor must acquire and develop is to follow through on James' exhortation to be "quick to listen." It will gain the love and appreciation of the local church. It will bless the particular individual. It will surely minister for Jesus and to Jesus.

What more can a pastor ask for?

CHAPTER 6

UNDERSTANDING THE MAKEUP
OF THE LOCAL CHURCH

Fellowship in many churches is more important than worship. That is not to endorse such an attitude, but it is to recognize the reality that feeling and being connected is vital for the functioning of the local church. This may be more true in the so-called non-liturgical churches, but even at that, the hunger to belong and be joined to others is an increasing feature of this post-modern age.

This is true in terms of the existing fellowship and it is even more true in a church committed to outreach, evangelism and discipling.

"Coffee hour" and its equivalents are the lifeblood of the church today. Theologians and others may argue about the appropriateness of this, but cannot dispute its reality. It is in these informal sessions that much of the pastoral ministry happens.

A learned colleague of mine argues that this is a product of Attention Deficit Disorder. He claims that this has reached epidemic proportions. Whether or not it is true, the reality remains. The kind of thing that coffee hour sets out to accomplish touches the very survival of the church.

The coffee hour in the church I attend is energetic, happy, even, to use a cliché, heart-warming. All over the hall people are engrossed in good-humoured talk.

They may be discussing the sermon, keeping one eye on their kids and the other on their friends. They may be graduating from the weather or politics to economics or family. Clearly they are enjoying what is happening. Most of them.

Is what we observe, in fact, happening? Social inter-action is clearly a positive. Everybody supports the concept. Is it really taking place?

The most superficial reading of the Gospels would indicate that Jesus did not just put in an appearance at social events, he participated in them to such an extent that he was criticized for enjoying wine and good food. John's introduction to the public ministry of Jesus was at a wedding, where Jesus' mother encouraged Him to do something about the inadequate supply of wine.

All that being said, there is another side to this.

First of all, there are the people who seldom, if ever, come to coffee hour or similar church social times. They step quickly out of church on Sunday mornings as soon as the benediction is pronounced. Some feel alienated and estranged, a condition that the New Testament is committed to heal. Christians are not excluded from citizenship. "In Christ Jesus you, who were once far away have been brought near by the blood of Christ." (Eph. 2:13) Some look almost haunted and have not experienced either what Paul speaks about when he says, "No longer strangers or foreigners" or what many who remain for a social time appear to have discovered.

"I never go to coffee hour," said one man in his mid-thirties. "They all seem so connected and make me feel even more that there is nobody I belong to." For him coffee hour is a metaphor for what others have that he would love to have but has found out of reach. He is still, emotionally if not theologically, "a stranger and foreigner."

In every community there are also people who are disillusioned with church. Whether or not their complaints are justified, the grievances are real to them. They find themselves unable to break into the social network of the church. It looks so attractive on the surface; undoubtedly it is so for those on the inside. However, there appears to be little room for them. For them, even to participate in a church gathering is the triumph of hope over experience.

Others may be thoughtful people who want to mull over the worship service on their own. They react negatively to what they perceive as the triviality of coffee hour. It seems, to them, dominated by superficial conversations and noisy children.

They are not really judgmental or overly pious, they just like silence and contemplation rather than an abundance of clamour. If the social time became a time of ministry some of these people maybe would be the first to be there.

How can we keep the social, fellowship values of a church gathering and make it a spiritual event?

In my church the pastor is given a pew card designed primarily for first-time visitors. An unfamiliar name on the card indicates a new arrival. The pastor phones the number provided.

Pastor: We were pleased to see you in church last Sunday and hope you felt at home and welcomed.

Contact: Thanks for calling. I did enjoy the service and appreciated what you were saying. Several people spoke to me afterwards.

Pastor: May I ask if you were able to stay for coffee and meet some other people?

Contact: I know staying afterward is a great way to meet people, but my experience of visiting after church is that it seems to distract me from the experience of worship. This is just me. It's probably not like that for others!

Pastor: I'm sorry that has been your experience. It certainly can be noisy, but there doesn't seem any other way of expressing fellowship and making general contact with people.

Contact: I don't have any solution, but for me a Bible study and home group might be more useful. Is that available?

Pastor: We have ten home groups at the moment. Let me research places, times and types of group, and I'll get back to you with some options

*   *   *

Men and women in this position scan the crowd. Occasionally someone apparently desirable and eligible looms in sight. The problem is how to make connections without being obvious. Quite a challenge in a small- or medium-sized church. A warm and caring church family can offer advice, security and encouragement when appropriate.

The hunger for intimacy is aroused by observing what appear to be happy casual conversations going on all around but not including the very people that such fellowship times were designed to reach. We have a real dilemma on our hands.

There is, of course, another huge issue we keep on confronting. How can we generate encounters that go beyond the surface concerns? Nobody wants to turn a fellowship time into a Freudian or a Rogerian session.

We have insisted that good human interaction focusing on the normal bits and pieces of our lives is both desirable and essential. Some banter, a little non-threatening and non-destructive gossip, along with a good deal of trivia is part of human exchange. But if it never gets beyond this, casual conversation becomes the curse of the local church.

This is true for a number of reasons.

It gives the impression that the Christian church is content with the superficial. All that is happening is that people are talking about matters that really are of little ultimate importance. They are either afraid, unwilling or unable to go any deeper. Does nobody ever need to talk about their real lives, the stuff that makes or breaks existence? In the midst of all the small talk is nobody crying out for serious conversations about serious issues?

Carl Roger's analogy of counselling as someone knocking at your front door applies. The new individual who arrives at a church function is, by simply by being there, knocking on the church's front door. The question is, will the person get beyond knocking?

Too often the conversation never gets beyond the front step. Someone knocking on your church door is hoping that you may actually extend an invitation to enter into your spiritual home. Unless you establish trust, the church door may be as far as that person will get.

There may be enough trust on both sides to invite a person into the "living room" of this spiritual home. Beyond that you may go together into the kitchen, which will be a bit messy but not totally embarrassing. Under very rare circumstances will you allow someone into the basement. It will take time and trust for this to happen.

The reason that "mere superficial conversations" are the curse of the local church is that people do get invited into the house, many even get as far as the living room but no further. That can be a huge tragedy. How big a tragedy can be perceived only if we become aware of who is actually there in church on a given Sunday, and the depth of the need and the searching for someone who is able to lead them to the healing of the Lord Jesus.

People in local churches have permitted me to have access to more than their living rooms. Nevertheless, I cannot help observing how they are relating in the brief conversations around church. It bears little or no resemblance to the often gut-wrenching issues they are confronting.

If they never have anything more than those superficial conversations they are going to feel more frustrated and indeed more alienated.

The reality is that we need to re-educate ourselves to the actual makeup of most local churches. There may have been a time in history when the "good" people were in the church and the "bad" people were not. More likely, the truth was simply better hidden than it is today. The appearance was of a congregation where everyone believed basically the same things. You could count on a uniform standard of behaviour, give or take a little. There are small pockets of churches, largely made up of elderly people, where this would still be true, but that is no longer the norm. Indeed the presence of people whose beliefs and behaviour are outside the Christian norm may be one of the critical signs of an alive church. Proverbs tells us, "Where no oxen are, the crib is clean" (Prov. 14:4).

This variety in beliefs and lifestyles in any congregation with a hundred members or more is both a challenge and an exhausting pastoral dilemma. Though this does not mean that churches no longer agree on basic beliefs, it does mean that the presence of a significant number of dissidents presents a problem.

To put it another way. In terms of the experience of family and a whole raft of other criteria, churches have been dramatically affected by the breakdown of the community. Fatherless in America reflects on this reality. "The United States is becoming an increasingly fatherless society." The author goes on to state, "Tonight, about 40 percent of American children will go to sleep in homes in which their fathers do not live."[39]

What is true in the United States is usually true of Canada and most of western society. It is sadly becoming equally true in the local church. The variety of family constellations is staggering: single-parent families, remarriage families, singles, widows, divorcees, as well as individuals who cohabit homosexually or heterosexually. There are divisions theologically, vocationally, sociologically, spiritually, et cetera. The amazing thing is that the church survives and sometimes thrives.

In the midst of all this, the pastoral concerns are staggering. We need to draw a more accurate profile of a medium-sized church.

There will hopefully be a range of ages from newborns to the elderly. There will be a variety of occupations, from the tradesperson and the entre-preneur to the academic and the professional. There will be people in vocational crisis and people who are successful. But that is only the beginning.

There will be at least one couple for whom gender issues complicate the relationship, to put it mildly. Whether the partner is aware or not, one of those in the apparently heterosexual relationship is gay. They have children and a place of significance in the church and community. They will not risk losing that.

The heterosexual partner may be willing to settle for this with the understanding that the gay partner is not sexually promiscuous. It is nevertheless a family secret, disclosed only to the pastor. It is difficult for them to cope with such a stressful reality along with the other challenges of marriage and teenage children. Issues of support and accountability are huge. The shadow of AIDS also hovers, as do the questions like what the partner may be fantasizing when they have intercourse, if and when they do. They bring a heavy agenda to the church service, though it would not be perceived by a superficial look.

There will be more than one couple affected by substance abuse of one kind or another. It may be a spouse or a teenage child with a drinking problem. It could be an addiction to prescription or illegal drugs. Trying to put a good face on things is the price to be paid to keep the family together and in church. At least if they are in church the possibility of a dramatic spiritual experience exists. They believe and hope. It had better come soon before the financial and personal problems tip the boat irreversibly.

Another family will be one that has been caught in corporate downsizing. The father was well established in middle to senior management with apparently unassailable job security. They could afford for the wife not to work outside the home. There was ample money for the summer cottage or the ski chalet. But no longer. The severance pay did not compensate for the emotional trauma and the threat to a comfortable way of life. He is asking, "Will I ever get a job anywhere near the one I've lost?" She is asking, "What did we do wrong and why is God putting us through this mess?" He further wonders if it is not just a job he has lost but potentially every-thing. "If I don't replace my income it will all go. The chalet, the cottage, the social position, the family, maybe even the marriage. What, in God's name, am I doing here in church. Does anyone really care? If God cares, what does He care about?"

Another couple come in separately and do not sit together. It is his turn to have the children, so they sit with him. The divorce is in process and everyone in that family feels uncomfortable, as do their friends.

An older female teenager is there. She has been experimenting sexually. Last night she had unprotected sex with a man she scarcely knows. "Will I get AIDS? What if I am pregnant? Is abortion an unforgivable sin?"

A couple of people have suffered with long-term clinical depression to the point of suicide. Some people with severe clinical depression are easy to identify, but others hide their condition as if it were AIDS. It is impossible to exaggerate the pain in such an individual's life. They appear to be functioning well in work and in family. But behind that appearance is someone who lives a life of tumultuous despair.

There are many other people in church on Sunday. There is the young adult who longs for at least some measure of human intimacy, but who comes and goes without it. There is the individual who pleaded with God for healing for herself or a family member. There was no apparent answer. There is the individual with all kinds of intellectual questions that not even Philip Yancey or C.S. Lewis have written about.

This ignores the man who has been taken to court over his step-daughter's allegations of sexual touching. The list could go on and on until it encompasses the entire congregation, perhaps to include the pastor. The pastor is not immune to life's marital, personal and sexual problems.

There may have been little in a given church service that spoke to the particular needs of that variety of people. A pastor who regularly prays through his church membership and who comes spiritually sensitive into the coffee hour will be ready for the Lord to direct his contacts. One of the greatest joys in the ministry is to look back with awe and gratitude on conversations in those circumstances that were overruled by the Spirit.

Some people would see this sketch of the makeup of the church as an exaggeration. They would be wrong. Indeed the truth likely is that it is understated. And pastoral care workers in chaplaincy or parachurch ministry are likely to encounter an equal or greater diversity.

What responsibilities has the church of Christ, and particularly pastoral care workers?

Evangelical churches tend to over-promise and under-deliver. This is not the fault of the gospel they preach, as much as their misinterpretation of it. When Paul describes his own emotional condition at times he is exceedingly frank. He refers to "weakness, and in fear, and much trembling" (1 Cor. 2:3).

Paul is not outlining a series of psychological and emotional problems like the ones I have described. But he is focusing on what comes close to emotional trauma. It at least indicates that Christians are not immune to the kinds of emotional extremes that affect the rest of humanity. The idea that the church is made up of people who have conquered all the emotional and spiritual swings in life is not true to experience; nor is it consistent with what we discover in the Bible, either in the Old Testament or New Testament.

How are we to cope with such variety, let alone be a healing ministry? Quite obviously many of the people described will need much more than a casual conversation lasting only a few minutes. The point is that the average congregation is made up of fallible, often emotionally fragile people as well as wilful sinners. It would take the energy and time of a host of people to minister to them.

Recruiting and training lay people is a clear and urgent priority, but when people are in trouble the first person they will likely contact outside their family group will be the minister. The initial contact will almost certainly occur as part of seemingly casual conversation in a casual setting. They will feel out the pastor to discover whether there is any sensitivity and willingness to be helpful. They will likely be experiencing deeply entrenched fears of rejection.

If there is an effort to get beyond that, it can be the beginning of real healing. This often will involve referring the person to other resource people. It will challenge the pastor to find lay people who will, out of their experiences, training and their own spiritual resources, be able to do this.

The pastor remains a key person in the process. This happens in a number of ways: by modelling a different kind of casual conversation, one that checks what is really at the heart of the particular communication; by being a discerning person who listens with a third ear to the Holy Spirit; by being aware of the professional resources in the church and community; by recruiting lay people who will do the work of ministry.

This will enrich the ministry of the local church and enhance the self-worth of all the people involved. Fellowship times will be transformed. Appearance and reality will come together. It will be an adventure for lay people who are trained and equipped to listen carefully. They will help people go beyond the superficialities. People in need will experience a caring church. The glacier of alienation will begin to melt. The power of the Spirit ministering through the body of believers will bring a sense of the presence of God.

People who come to coffee hour will not want to go home. Why should they? They have found home in church in the best sense.

It is beyond reason to expect that many of the problems outlined here will be resolved in five minutes or less! But surely it is not beyond reason to expect that we can anticipate a modest beginning. We can instil confidence that this is a church where people who feel alienated and rejected can see a glimmer of hope that their perception is not so.

The attitude and reaction of the pastor can, at least, model that of Jesus in John 4 and John 8. He was clearly non-judgmental toward the woman "caught in adultery" and the Samaritan woman married five times and currently cohabiting.

Non-judgmental he was, but that must not be confused with being *permissive.* The judgmental church and pastor violate the needy person. But reactions need to be balanced by an unwillingness to respond in such a way that ends up reinforcing behaviour that is both unbiblical and destructive.

Pastoral workers need to resist the idea that they have, or are expected to have, a solution to all the problems outlined. They need to read and reread Gerard Egan's *The Skilled Helper*.[40]

But the best informed, best equipped, best educated and most deeply spiritual pastor will still be daunted by the challenge. The answer to the question, Who is sufficient for these things? is always "Our sufficiency is of God."

Listening to people expressing their deepest needs, listening to what the Spirit has to say, involving the body of believers who believe in the power of prayer and are committed to Scripture is the heart of all we do in church.

It is an exciting and fulfilling ministry.

CHAPTER 7

REVOLUTIONIZING PASTORAL CARE
IN THE POST-MODERN AGE

I t is a bit of a puzzle to figure out why the brief conversation has fallen into such a black hole. It has been, directly and indirectly, the nuts and bolts of pastoral contact since the days of our Lord, including our Lord himself.

This has been true not only of the pastoral involvement of clergy but also of lay commitment. In any local church at any given time there have been people, with or without official standing, to whom church members have gone for advice and prayer. They would often be approached, usually with the appearance of a casual conversation, as soon as church was over.

"May I ask you what you think about . . . ?" is a typical question addressed to a respected church leader or elder. Or the elder may take the initiative and ask, "May I ask you how you are doing?"

The church member would sometimes report to

others, "I talked to so-and-so yesterday and he said. . . . That was very helpful"

These would nearly always be brief encounters. Contact with the pastor would regularly be of a similar nature. It might lead to a more intensive discussion. Or it might require a recommendation to talk to some kind of a professional. But it would initially be brief.

The practice of confession as the core element in Catholic pastoral care for centuries is an example of this. At its worst it was a theological and emotional disaster. But at its best it was direct, immediate and brief. It mediated a word from the Lord.

The Presbyterian minister at the church my mother, brother and sister attended in my childhood would advertise his calling schedule. Right on time he would knock on our door. He would make a little social chatter. He would read from the Bible and pray. He would come and go in less than ten minutes. Yet his visit was eagerly awaited and it was chewed over afterward. To have him pray for each of us by name created an impression on me that I remember to this very day.

Without doubt, that fractured family of origin of mine needed much more than such a short visit. The failure to provide for this is a cause for justifiable complaint. Nevertheless, it still had significance. He, astonishingly, brought to that troubled household a sense of the presence and care of God.

Such a process would be almost unknown today. Pastors rarely make regular house calls. Are the few minutes at coffee hour and other similar occasions a post-modern equivalent? Yes and No.

Another approach is to ask whether we can convey the presence of God in a very limited time frame?

The hospital chaplain's life and ministry is dominated by the hospital schedule. Is the crucial question for the chaplain, How much time do I have? If that is the question, little of value will be accomplished. If the question is, How can I be Christ for this person? the whole dynamic changes.

Hospital chaplains work under all kinds of constraints. The process of treatment, the prognosis, the hospital staff, who can be anything from covertly hostile to avidly cheerful, the presence of family—all this and more affect the visit. That is to say nothing about the patient's religious history, present circumstances and serious anxieties. All this and the spiritual and emotional state of the chaplain are calculated to do violence to the actual visit and contact.

In spite of all this, an effective chaplain can and does mediate the presence of God that is vital in any sense of ministering to the whole person. Respecting the realities of the particular situation is a given. Being a careful observer goes without question. The chaplain must be able to read all that is going on. All these elements of good attending skills should be in place and be developing. The chaplain needs, more than all else, to have imprinted on his or her very being the words of Jesus, "I was sick and you visited me" (Matt. 25:36).

If the hospital chaplain can accomplish useful work in such pressured circumstances, is it unreasonable to ask the same of the pastor in the constraints of the pastoral setting?

The pastoral counselling movement came into being out of a number of concerns. There was an awareness that in many church situations people were being grievously shortchanged. For the majority of people the experience of conversion did not, in itself, resolve all their problems. When they presented their continuing problems to the pastor they were too often put off with a quotation from the Bible and a brief prayer. It did not prove effective.

There was, in addition, an avalanche of knowledge on human dynamics. Some of this was anti-Christian but some appeared compatible with Scripture.

A consequence was a major change in the whole concept of pastoral care. The style and content changed dramatically. Any attempt to deal with human problems that did not consume a number of sessions, each lasting at least fifty minutes, was not simply inadequate it was positively dangerous to the church member. The church member became the client and the pastor became the great physician and psychologist.

We seem to be involved in another paradigm shift. The emphasis is changing again in many circles. There is a double reality at work. The amount of perceived available time at the disposal of the pastor, and indeed the church member, has almost disappeared. There is not enough time in any given week to do the pastoral care in fifty-minute blocks. It is mathematically impossible to find the time to care for a medium-sized church on that basis. Indeed, even if the time were available to the pastor, most church members would not be willing to make use of it. They have enough time, as they perceive it, for a brief conversation. If something happens in that conversation that uncovers a deeper need, then more serious conversation will likely be possible.

In North America the accepted demands of modern family life are close to being destructive to the family. The combination of sport, culture, school and family ambition, as well as the perceived need for double incomes are overwhelming the institution. There certainly needs to be more time for church-related activities and contact. Otherwise the spiritual becomes marginalized.

Recognizing the reality of all of this is not to be understood as supporting it. It is motivating the attempt to find a constructive way of working around it. There should also be some attempt to encourage radical changes of outlook and practice. Spiritual concerns need to be aired. The disciplines of relevant Scripture and prayer are vital. Pastoral time spent on occasional family visits where children are included is important. But, alas, in our modern world this is forgotten.

If modern church life is under considerable and disturbing time pressures, there is equally similar pressure on the secular therapist. In some cases the unwillingness of insurance companies to pay for unlimited counselling has quite remarkably condensed the number of sessions.

The five-minute-or-less conversation satisfies the modern, pressurized life style. It also opens up the opportunity for a more prolonged dialogue and, when desirable, a referral.

It is not therefore "either . . . or," but "both . . . and."

Five minutes of casual conversation are usually enough to give both parties a sense of whether that is all that is wanted or needed, or if much more serious issues require attention.

There is also a growing model of Solution Oriented Brief Therapy (SOBT) that is impatient with the older model. The focus is on solutions not on problems. It describes itself as "a revolutionary and rapid program for staying together." It would be a caricature of SOBT to give the impression that five minutes or less is all that is required to fix a troubled marriage or any other emotional problem, but the paradigm of long-term counselling is changing. The process of identifying the issue and setting clear goals is speeding up. Many people do not want, need or require long-term counselling. They often have a single issue they want to surface with a mature and discerning fellow believer and would like some immediate feedback. It is not inappropriate to give it.

Allied with SOBT is cognitive therapy's ABC approach (Activating event, Belief system, emotional Consequence). The argument is that the activating event is not the direct cause of the emotional reaction. The real cause is in the client's belief system. If that can be classified and changed, real progress will be made quite quickly.

During a coffee break with a pastoral colleague, he raised a concern about a staff person for whom he was responsible. He described a person who was capable and gifted but who "fell apart emotionally" on being the recipient of even moderate criticism, even though it was given within a positive context. "He doesn't come into work," complained my colleague. "He has a short-term depression. What is going on? How can I help him?"

We went through the ABC approach.

The activating event was criticism that devastated him. The appearance was that the criticism caused the emotional response. But this criticism was moderate and he was given quite a lot of positive feedback.

The idea that it was the way the activating event triggered his negative belief system and caused the reaction was fresh and new to my colleague. "Can you help him identify what he says to himself when this kind of thing happens?" I asked. "Instead of focusing on his reactions, it is more helpful to discover with him his negative beliefs about life, himself and the Lord. What you can help him change are the negative beliefs he falls back on." No doubt my friend will use this with his colleague.

Incidentally, it is also an interesting exercise at a pastoral staff meeting to persuade people to identify their real belief system and how it impacts them. It is even more valuable for them to look at biblical and life-affirming alternatives.

The conversation with my friend on this particular issue was a fragment of the time spent over coffee. It was enough to introduce him to a new approach. Hopefully it was sufficient to make sure he would not do more harm than good. But I knew he was a sufficiently caring person to not deal with his colleague in a bull-headed way.

The use of this concept illustrates the way secular ideas about therapy, can and do, influence how the pastor ministers in day-to-day situations. The connection can be brief and it can open a door in someone's mind that can lead to a higher degree of self understanding and long-term change.

Therapists and pastors are not alone in finding ways to deal with the kinds of problems that are epidemic in our society.

One of the surprises in checking out the material in this book has been the reaction of people professionally involved in the care of others. The model of the multiple fifty-minute counselling session is very well established. The likelihood of very brief encounters being productive ought to produce scorn if not contempt.

Quite the opposite has been the case. There has been little resistance and almost no rejection. This has been true across the board. Pastors, chaplains and mental health professionals of various kinds have all supported the idea, if not the practice.

A psychiatrist friend enquired if I was familiar with the BATHE technique. It is an attempt to give primary care physicians a verbal procedure that will enable them to help patients.

The amount of time this process requires is greater than the five-minute limit we have suggested but is considerably less than the more normal fifty minutes.

Basically the purpose of the BATHE technique is to help patients understand their own problems and know that they can handle them. It is eminently suitable for patients who are facing moderate difficulties. It is not designed for patients who are in severe pain, life-threatening circumstances or those who are facing serious problems, such as suicidal patients, battered spouses, sexual abuse victims, substance abuse and many others.

The BATHE technique consists of a series of four questions followed by an empathetic response.

Background: *What is going on in your life?*

Affect: *How do you feel about that?*

Trouble: *What troubles you most about that?*

Handling: *How are you handling that?*

Empathy: *That must be very difficult!*

The model is valuable in the context of the concerns of this book. A busy family doctor will be unable to give every patient hours of counselling, indeed is likely poorly trained for that. But the doctor can open up a process and help the patient understand where he or she is coming from. The doctor understands that it is not suitable or appropriate when there are serious psychiatric problems. Yet, for probably the majority of patients, it can be very productive.

There is obviously a difference between a doctor-patient relationship and a pastor-church member relationship. In the former, the individual has come to the doctor with a specific problem that the doctor is expected to solve. This gives the doctor both the right and obligation to ask very direct and otherwise intrusive questions.

It would not often be appropriate for the pastor to approach a person during a fellowship time and abruptly ask, "What is going on in your life?"

However, if the circumstances justified it, the pastor could ask permission to ask the question.

Pastor: Hi! It is great to see you here today.

Contact: Thanks, I am not feeling at all great today.

Pastor: I'm sorry to hear that.

Contact: You are not as sorry as I am! Things are not looking very good to me.

Pastor: May I ask you what is going on in your life that makes you say that?

Contact: It's a long story. Do you have time right now?

Pastor: At least we have time to get started. If we need more time we will find some.

Proponents of the BATHE questions insist on a number of important qualifications. They require more discipline than most doctors and pastors seem to possess.

For example, physicians are encouraged to say nothing except the BATHE questions. There should be no attempt to analyze or interpret the response. The desire to give advice should be resisted. There is permission to summarize and go on to the next question. The patient should be encouraged to answer the questions without much detail. Two minutes is the ration of time for the first question. Ten minutes for the whole process.

A detailed study of the questions and the approach behind BATHE could be helpful to the pastoral worker. It is, of course, vital to make sure that the pastor does not come across in a heavy-handed fashion.

The overall goal of the BATHE technique is to convince the patient that he or she can handle the problem. The technique does allow for some modifications. There is a recognition that gender can present difficulties. Male pastors and the local church have been very slow to understand that the male pastor relating to a female church member is not always appropriate.

Proponents point out that "it is very common to feel the interviewer has done nothing for the patient at the conclusion of the BATHE technique." They go on to add, "There is no need to modify anything about the technique in this situation. The physician must wait for the technique to percolate within the patient until the next office visit and then repeat the BATHE technique."

The procedure is a helpful way to encourage patients to clarify and understand their own lives. It concludes with the empathetic reassurance "That must be very difficult."

The reminder is crucial. "Recognize that it is not your job to fix the patient's problems only to provide support and clarification."

At the close of the session it is understood that this is, for some people, only the beginning of the process. The doctor may very well say "This is the type of problem that people often want to talk about with a counsellor. Would you like to pursue this further, either with a counsellor or with me next time you are here?"

The initiative is still with the patient, who can choose which alternative seems best, but it keeps the issue of constructive referral on the agenda.

The discerning pastor will note that this is very much a secular model. But it certainly does not preclude being aware of spiritual issues and concerns. Indeed these may very well dominate the response to the four BATHE questions.

Pastor: I noticed you during the worship service. You did not seem your usual self. You looked quite troubled and disconnected. That is not like you at all.

Contact: Was it as obvious as that? I certainly didn't mean to distract you from the sermon!"

Pastor: It was not quite as bad as that! But I did feel that you were quite preoccupied and finding it unusually difficult to focus. Would you be upset with me if I were to ask you what is going on in your life that is troubling you?

Contact: What is going on in my life? That is a very big question. My job looks as if it is going to be terminated. I have no idea what I will do. They will give me minimum severance. I am in my mid fifties. Who wants somebody that age? I am terrified at the prospect. Other people, I know, in this society have survived but it is a huge disaster for me.

Pastor: It almost seems banal to ask you how you feel about it?

Contact: Terrified. Alone. Scared. I wonder if I will ever work for a living again. It is not just the money. It's the feeling of being obsolete, a has been, somebody to be a figure of pity. Sounds full of maudlin self pity doesn't it?

Pastor: It sounds to me like somebody who is at the end of his emotional rope. I would like to hear more about it. This is not a good place for that kind of conversation. Can we find a time to get together?

Contact: I'd like that. I need to talk with somebody.

It is not really possible to give a particular individual all the immediate time he or she might need under these circumstances. This individual obviously requires significant time as soon as possible. Because of all the other people who may need the pastor's attention in that particular context a judgment must be made. At the least an appointment must be secured for later that day or as soon as is helpful for both parties.

That is not to indicate that there are not occasions when it will be right to abandon everything and give that person whatever time is necessary. This incident certainly comes close to such an occasion.

The reality of pastoral care in this post-modern age is also that the demand not only exceeds the supply but puts pressure on the pastor, whose available time and training are limited. The capacity to train lay people and the development of understanding resources in the community is essential.

There are a multitude of examples of this happening productively.

Maybe we need to take a leaf out of the book from the church that McManus describes. Father Dick McGinnis, the 58-year-old Rector of St. David's Episcopal Church in Jacksonville, Florida, was frustrated by the marital breakdowns in his church and the demands put upon him.

He asked a particular group of people to meet with him. They were to be those "whose marriages have been on the rocks but who have successfully come off of them—people who have been in extreme difficulty and have threatened divorce but are now in recovery."[41]

So began a wonderful productive lay experiment that recruited people who impacted the reconciliation process in marriages in that church. "There have been no divorces in the church since 1987 among those who have asked for help."

The model of marital and family counselling in the United Kingdom is RELATE. This is entirely a lay-recruited and lay-trained group of people. The most successful people dealing with alcoholism is Alcoholics Anonymous. Again this is an entirely lay organization. McGinnis uses an amended version of the ten steps in his approach.

Self awareness and the Spirit-filled wisdom of the congregation should be put to work. It would be invaluable find someone in the congregation who has counselling skills and do some role playing with them.

A more revolutionary approach would be to circulate a revised form of the ten-question checklist in chapter 4 to get congregational reaction. That would be a high-risk venture. Very scary!

Another practical approach would be to have someone with good counselling skills conduct a workshop based on Egan's *Skilled Helper.* It would be very important to make sure that such a person is comfortable with question 10 and endorses it.

The rewards for all of this are immense, especially in the training of lay people, many of whom are willing and anxious to participate. These would help change enough people in the church to produce a paradigm shift in pastoral care in any church.

The emphasis on the role of the pastor is not simply to enhance the pastor's awareness and skill level. It is because if the pastor does not understand all this the pastor will become the "cork in the bottle." When the pastor is on board, that will begin to create an ethos in the church that will change attitudes and people.

In the end it will lessen the pastor's pressures not increase them. Ironic, is it not!

There are a number of training programs available, including the Stephens Ministry and Marriage Encounter as well as other lay counselling movements. *Lay Counselling, Equipping Christians for a Helping Ministry* by Siang-Yang Tan is the "bible" of the lay counselling movement. In his introduction, Gary R. Collins notes, "This new book is a thoroughly documented, realistic, practical, relevant, psychologically sound, biblically based survey of the field of lay counselling. The author shows a clear sensitivity to the needs of the local church, and an awareness of denominational and cross-cultural differences."[42]

In the larger church it may be possible and desirable to set up a professional counselling service. It would multiply its effectiveness if a high proportion of time were to be used to train lay people.

The continual reality for the pastor who cares deeply for people is that he or she does not have the skills to deal with the complexity of the issues presented. The pastoral worker needs to have a realistic view of where his or her skills lie and perhaps even more importantly, where they do not. The pressure of time available and skills acquired make it highly desirable that the pastor learns how and when to refer.

Gary Collins makes the point that "no one person is skilled enough to counsel everyone, and referral is often a way to show your desire to have the counsellee get the best help possible.[43]

The pastor may in fact be asked directly by the church member for the name and telephone number of a practitioner in a particular discipline. "We are going through a bad patch in our marriage. Can you give me the name of a good marriage counsellor?" Provided the pastor has acquired a resource list, that question can easily be answered.

Sometimes the problem presented is one the pastor is expected to be competent to deal with. Defining what it means "to deal with it" is difficult anyway; it is exacerbated when the expectations are going to be disappointed.

It is always important that referral should not be seen as rejection. When referral is necessary because of lack of skill, it is desirable to be quite candid.

> **Pastor:** That is a difficult problem you're facing. It is not one in which I have much expertise. Would you like me to find someone in the community who can be helpful? I would really appreciate it if you would let me know how helpful that person is. Do please keep me in touch with how it is working out, if you decide to use her. Are you comfortable with this?"

One of the more controversial concerns in referral is the spiritual state of the person recommended. In a perfect world there would be sufficient people who are competent professionally and devout in their faith. However, in a perfect world you would not require such assistance!

Collins points out, "Many problems (medical issues, for example, or learning disorders) do not need to be treated by a Christian. Some psychological problems are far removed from Christian values and can be effectively handled by non-believers."

In the event that this referral is to someone who is a non-believer, it would be prudent to let the church member know that if the non-believer comes across as unsympathetic to matters of faith you would be happy to discuss that concern.

It is a much more complicated world compared with

that of the Presbyterian minister who called on our family. We have gone through a roller coaster on the issues of pastoral care. Indeed it seems as if the pastor is juggling half a dozen models of pastoral care, often with little or no apparent theological or biblical reflection.

What is being argued here is that if very limited time is a factor, that time can still be productive. It can signal support and it can begin the process of clarification. If the pastor is a genuinely godly person with well-developed attending skills, it can do much more.

It will be enough for some people. It will be the start of something for others. It will provide genuine human contact for many. It will mediate the presence of God for those open to receive Him.

All these are immense gains in a rushed, impersonal post-modern society. They also can represent pastoral care at its best, new or old.

Notes

1. Gerard Egan, *The Skilled Helper* (Brooks/Cole Publishing 1986) p. 3.

2. Ibid. p. 71.

3. David Martyn Lloyd-Jones, *Banner of Truth Trust,* Ian H. Murray, 1990.

4. Ibid., p. 407.

5 Ibid.

5. Ibid.

6. Ibid., p. 409.

7. George Sayer, *Jack: C.S. Lewis and His Times* (Macmillan, London, 1988).

8. Ibid., p. 132.

9. Ibid.

10. Ibid. p. 133.

11. Michele Weiner-Davis, *Fire Your Shrink* (New York: Simon & Schuster, 1995), p. 13.

12. Ibid.

13. Ibid., p. 14.

14. Michelle Weiner-Davis, *Divorce Busting* (New York: Simon & Schuster, 1992), p. 97.

15. Michael J. McManus, *Marriage Savers* (Grand Rapids: Zondervan, 1993).

16. Donald Capps, "Sex in the Parish: Social Scientific Explanation for why it Occurs," *Journal of Pastoral Care* 47 (Winter 1993), p. 354.

17. Shad Helmstetter, *What to Say When You Talk to Yourself* (London: Thorsons, 1991).

18. Ibid., p. 46.

19. Albert Ellis and J. Whitely (eds.), "Towards a New theory of Personalities" in *Theoretical and Empirical Foundations of Rational Emotive Thoughts* (Pacific Grove: Brooks/Cole, 1979), pp. 7–32, quoted in Gerald Corey, *Theory and Practice of Counseling and Psychotherapy* (Pacific Grove: Brooks/Cole, 1991), p. 329.

20. Ibid.

21.Gerald Corey, *Theory and Practice of Counseling and Psychotherapy* (Pacific Grove: Brooks/Cole, 1991), p. 329.

22. Gerard Egan, *The Skilled Helper* (Pacific Grove: Brooks/Cole Publishing, 1986), p. 79.

23. Ibid.

24. Ibid., p. 82.

25. Daniel Coleman, *Emotional Intelligence* (New York: Bantam Books, 1995), and *Working with Emotional Intelligence* (New York: Bantam Books, 1998).

26. *Working with Emotional Intelligence*, p. 317.

27. Ibid., 16.

28. Ibid., p. 317.

29. Ibid., p. 318

30. Ibid., p. 7.

31. Peter Davids, *Commentary on James* (Grand Rapids: William B. Eerdmans Publishing Company, 1982), p. 91.

32. Kathleen Norris, *The Cloister Walk* (New York: Riverhead Books, 1996), p. 143.

33. Gerard Egan, *The Skilled Helper* (Pacific Grove: Brooks/Cole Publishing Company, 1986).

34. Ibid., p. 88.

35. Ibid., p. 93.

36. Ibid.

37. Leon Morris, Tyndale New Testament Commentaries, *1 Corinthians* (Grand Rapids: Eerdmans, 1958), p. 60.

38. Gordon Fee, The New International Commentary on the New Testament, *The First Epistle to the Corinthians* (Grand Rapids: William B. Eerdmans, 1987), p. 117.

39. David Blankenhorn, *Fatherless America* (New York, NY: Basic Books, 1995) p. 1.

40. Gerard Egan, *The Skilled Helper* (Pacific Grove: Brooks/Cole Publishing, 1986).

41. Michael J. McManus, *Marriage Savers* (Grand Rapids, Mich: Zondervan, 1995), p. 201.

42. Siang-Yang Tan, *Lay Counselling, Equipping Christians for a Helping Ministry* (Zondervan 1991) p. 9.

43. Gary R. Collins, *Christian Counseling* (Word Publishing 1989) p. 70.

Printed in the United States
1349100001B/562-570

9 781573 832311